Cambridge checkpoint

THIRD EDITION

Lower Secondary
English

8

John Reynolds

HODDER
EDUCATION
AN HACHETTE UK COMPANY

Orders: please contact Hachette UK Distribution, Hely Hutchinson Centre, Milton Road, Didcot, Oxfordshire, OX11 7HH. Telephone: +44 (0)1235 827827. Email education@hachette.co.uk Lines are open from 9 a.m. to 5 p.m., Monday to Friday.

ISBN: 978 1 3983 0184 9

© John Reynolds 2022

First published in 2011

This edition published in 2022 by

Hodder Education,

An Hachette UK Company

Carmelite House

50 Victoria Embankment

London EC4Y 0DZ

www.hoddereducation.com

Impression number 10 9 8 7 6 5 4 3 2 1

Year 2025 2024 2023 2022 2021

Cover photo © peangdao - stock.adobe.com

Illustrations by Oxford Designers and Illustrators and Abigael Cassell

Typeset by Ian Foulis Design, Saltash, Cornwall

Printed in Italy

A catalogue record for this title is available from the British Library.

Contents

Introduction

Cambridge Checkpoint Lower Secondary English Student's Book 8 is the second in a series of three books designed to cover the Cambridge Lower Secondary English curriculum framework.

This Student's Book will build on the key skills and types of texts you met in Stage 7, building up your vocabulary, diving deeper into a range of texts and writers, and providing lots of opportunities to practise and consolidate your English skills through a range of group work and individual activities.

We hope the work you do in this book will be enjoyable and challenging, whether it sets you up for further study in English or provides valuable practice for your use of English in everyday situations.

You will cover a range of activities to practise your reading, writing, speaking and listening skills.

Each chapter also contains key skills sections which home in on a specific topic. Some of these may be revision activities, such as revisiting grammar or sentence types, but some may introduce newer areas of learning such as creating a distinctive diary entry. The texts and activities become more challenging as you work through each book to match your growing understanding of English.

You will find a variety of genres in the reading texts, drawn from a range of cultures, geographical locations and authorial voices. There should be something interesting here for everybody and you may find new styles of writing you haven't encountered before!

We hope you enjoy the exercises and activities in this book alongside your studies of Cambridge Lower Secondary English. Ask for help if you need it but try hard first. Studying English stretches and develops your skill set and it can be very rewarding!

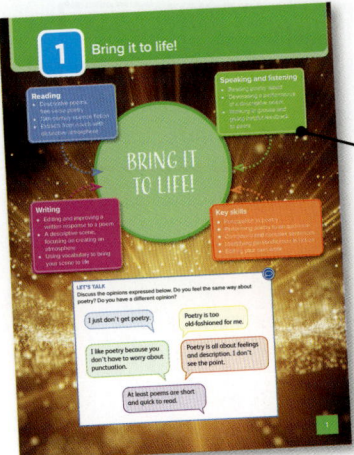

How to use this book

The *chapter opener* pages give you a snapshot of all the exciting reading, writing, speaking and listening skills you will practise in the chapter, along with the key skill(s) you will focus on, and introduce the new topic with a discussion.

Activity

These boxes allow you to explore and practise skills in pairs or groups.

EXERCISE

These boxes allow you to practise and consolidate skills on your own.

Author, poet or playwright

These boxes provide extra information about the creators of texts. This is often useful when a text has been created in a particular social, historical or political context.

KEY WORDS

These boxes explain all the literary and grammar terms. The key words are repeated in the glossary pages at the back of the book for easy revision.

LET'S TALK

These activities offer opportunities to discuss the content in pairs, groups or as a class.

Spelling

These boxes encourage you to think about the spelling rules and patterns you have learned in previous stages.

These boxes ask questions for you to think about as you read through the texts. You may prefer to try answering these on your second or third reading or after attempting the activities or extracts.

Spotlight on

These boxes ask you to think about specific aspects of the text, such as purpose, audience, historical context and theme.

WORD ATTACK SKILLS

These boxes ask you to look at vocabulary and language in context. This includes working out the meaning of unfamiliar words, looking at a writer's choice of language and discussing linguistic and literary techniques.

HINT

These boxes guide you to think about specific things.

The *Reviewing* section at the end of each chapter lets you evaluate the texts you have read, suggests similar or contrasting texts for further reading and asks you to reflect on your learning in the chapter.

This means that there is a listening activity. All audio is available to download for free from www.hoddereducation.com/cambridgeextras

EXTENSION

These are more demanding tasks or tasks that help you to practise a wider range of skills.

GLOSSARY

This box gives you the meaning of any words from the text that may be new or challenging.

Do you remember?

Find a quick reminder about things you should already have learned in these features.

DID YOU KNOW?

Discover interesting facts in these boxes.

The reading cycle

Follow these three steps to read actively:

1 Before reading

It may sound silly to prepare your brain to read a text, but knowing what the text type or genre is and what subject you are reading about helps you to comprehend what you read and to make connections to past learning and/or experiences.

- Look for clues about the text type or genre.
- Read the title and subtitle to find out what the text is about.
- Use skimming and scanning techniques to look for:
  - the layout of the text
  - heading levels and/or numbering of headings or subheadings
  - emphasis given through the use of different colours, key words, italics or bold
  - artwork, illustrations and/or photographs and their captions
  - graphics and graphs, diagrams, charts or maps
  - key words or specific details.

2 During reading

These activities will help you to analyse the structure and language features in more detail.

- Use the Word Attack Skills boxes to work out the meaning of words using contextual clues, the word families they are from, the morphology or root of the words.
- Ask questions while you read. Use the questions that appear alongside the texts.
- Make notes of main and supporting ideas.
- Visualise what is being described (particularly in descriptive writing).
- Pay attention to the way the creator of the text has used language and grammar to enhance the meaning in texts and to create effects.

3 After reading

These activities will help you to understand the meaning of the text.

- Think about the purpose and audience of the text. What was it supposed to do? Who was it written for?
- Evaluate the impact of the text on you. What is your opinion of the text?
- Evaluate and discuss different interpretations of the text.
- Think about texts that are similar to, or contrast with, the text.
- Exercise critical language awareness:
  - Distinguish between facts and opinions.
  - Compare direct (explicit) and implied (implicit) information and meaning.
  - Determine the social, political and cultural background of texts.
  - Identify emotive and manipulative language such as stereotyping and bias.

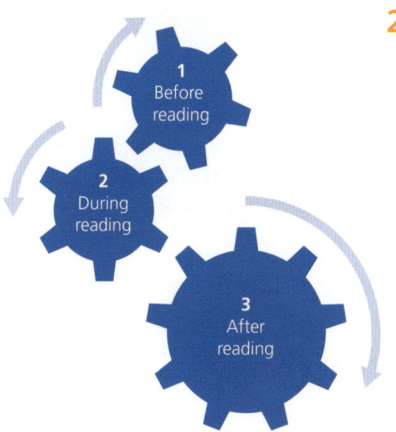

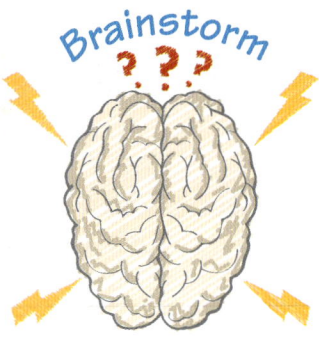

The writing cycle

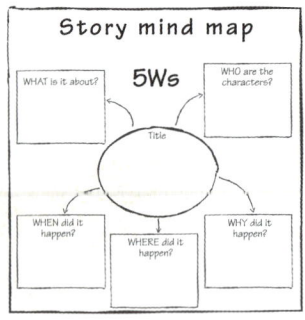

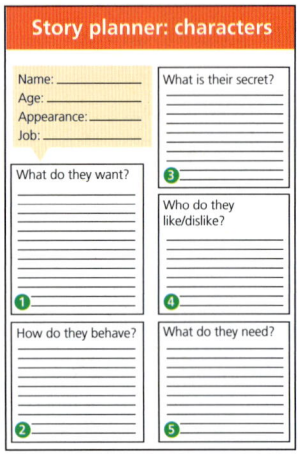

1 Generate ideas by brainstorming, writing your ideas on paper or talking with others or doing research. Think about:
   - your audience – who will read your work? Who is your text for?
   - the intended purpose of your writing – is it to entertain, inform, persuade or a combination of those things?
   - the writing features you will use to suit the text type or genre.

2 Organise your ideas by planning your writing.
   - Use different planning methods to shape your ideas, such as a mind map, a storyboard or an online template.

3 Write a draft. Think about:
   - the tone and register (formal or informal) you should use (see page 74)
   - developing distinctive voices for your characters.

4 Revise your draft. Think about:
   - the types of sentences you could use: simple, compound (page 16) or, complex (page 16) sentences and using different types of sentences to avoid monotony
   - the range of punctuation you could use: colons (page 5), semi-colons (page 5) or dashes (page 5)
   - using appropriate connectives or beginning sentences with interesting connectives (page 16)
   - the range of language you could use to make your writing more interesting, such as using better adjectives or adverbs (page 83).

5 Edit your writing.
   - Evaluate your writing by checking your language, grammar, spelling and the structure of your writing.
   - Ask a partner to read your writing and do the same.
   - Correct any mistakes.

6 Proofread your writing.
   - Rewrite or type your work. Think about different layouts and decide which one will best suit your purpose: handwritten, printed or onscreen.
   - Read through your work carefully to make sure that you have corrected all your mistakes.

7 Present your writing.

1 Bring it to life!

Reading
* Descriptive poems, free-verse poetry
* 19th-century science fiction
* Extracts from novels with distinctive atmosphere

Speaking and listening
* Reading poetry aloud
* Developing a performance of a descriptive poem
* Working in groups and giving helpful feedback to peers

BRING IT TO LIFE!

Writing
* Editing and improving a written response to a poem
* A descriptive scene, focusing on creating an atmosphere
* Using vocabulary to bring your scene to life

Key skills
* Punctuation in poetry
* Performing poetry to an audience
* Compound and complex sentences
* Identifying personification in fiction
* Editing your own work

LET'S TALK

Discuss the opinions expressed below. Do you feel the same way about poetry? Do you have a different opinion?

> I just don't get poetry.

> Poetry is too old-fashioned for me.

> I like poetry because you don't have to worry about punctuation.

> Poetry is all about feelings and description. I don't see the point.

> At least poems are short and quick to read.

Speaking and listening

Describing a scene

1 Work with a partner. Look for the details in the street scenes below and share your insights and observations with each other.
   - What do you notice?
   - What do you wonder?
   - What does it remind you of?
   - Try to imagine what stories are in the lives of the people in the scene.
   - What would it be like to arrive in this street and walk along it?
   - Try to hear the noises, the shouts or whispers. What other sensations might there be? Are you jostled in the crowd?

2 Now work on your own. Imagine yourself on a street you know well. It could be a street where you go shopping, or part of your route to school. Look at the familiar people and surroundings with fresh eyes and curiosity. Who do you see? What are the sounds in the background?

3 Join your partner again or work in a small group to discuss your street scene.
   - What do you see and hear in the street?
   - What do you see but not really notice?
   - Who is there, and what activities are going on?

Reading

Using poetry to describe a scene

You are going to read a poem about a street scene. The poet has stopped in the street, where a knife-grinder is at work. The poet is curious about what he sees and hears.

GLOSSARY

livelong – entire (of a long period of time)

curb – kerb

knife-grinder – someone who sharpens the edge of a knife by pressing it against a spinning stone wheel, which is powered by his feet

tread – step

forth issue – to come out of something

effusing – moving around in a loose way

unminded – ignored

diffusing – spreading over a wide area

Poet: Walt Whitman

Walt Whitman was an American poet (1819-92). This poem, 'Sparkles from the Wheel', comes from his ground-breaking first collection of poems, *Leaves of Grass*. He wrote in **free verse**, a new form of poetry at the time.

'Sparkles from the Wheel'

Where the city's ceaseless crowd moves on the **livelong** day,
Withdrawn, I join a group of children watching – I pause aside with them.

By the **curb**, toward the edge of the flagging,
A **knife-grinder** works at his wheel, sharpening a great knife;
Bending over, he carefully holds it to the stone – by foot and knee,
With **measur'd tread**, he turns rapidly – As he presses with light but firm hand,
Forth issue, then, in **copious** golden jets,
Sparkles from the wheel.

The scene, and all its belongings – how they seize and affect me!
The sad, sharp-**chinn'd** old man, with worn clothes, and broad shoulder-band of leather;
Myself, **effusing** and fluid – a phantom curiously floating – now here **absorb'd** and arrested;

The group, (an **unminded** point, set in a vast surrounding;)
The attentive, quiet children – the loud, proud, **restive** base of the streets;
The low, **hoarse** purr of the whirling stone – the light-**press'd** blade,
Diffusing, dropping, sideways-darting, in tiny showers of gold,
Sparkles from the wheel.

Walt Whitman

WORD ATTACK SKILLS

Find these words in the poem. Suggest possible meanings, then research their definitions.

✔ copious
✔ restive
✔ hoarse

Spelling

Some poets use contractions (words where letters are removed and replaced by an **apostrophe**). This is sometimes done to reduce the number of **syllables** in a word and in the past was often done to words ending in 'ed' where the 'ed' used to be pronounced as a separate syllable. There are four examples in this poem: measur'd, chinn'd, absorb'd and press'd.

HINT

Poems are full of detail and the language often zings with many ideas all at once. It is difficult to take it all in. Don't worry – many people feel like this when reading a poem for the first time.

Activity 1.2

Work in a group and build some shared understanding of the poem.

1 Discuss and answer these questions.
- What does the title of the poem refer to? Where do the sparkles come from?
- It's a street scene. Who is in the street? Who is watching the knife-grinder?
- The knife-grinder is working. What actions are involved?
- There is a hint in the poem about what the knife-grinder looks like. What are we told about him?
- What is so interesting to everyone gathered around the knife-grinder?
- The poet has noticed a group who have stopped to watch. Who is in the crowd, and why has the knife-grinder got their attention?

2 We often use 'arrested' when a person is caught by police, but it can simply mean 'stopped'. Find 'arrested' in the poem. Which sense (meaning) do you think it has here in the poem?

3 What does 'the edge of the flagging' mean?

4 The word 'measur'd' is used in an unfamiliar way. Find it in the poem and think about the possible meaning of the word in this context.

EXTENSION

Although the poem was written long before movies were invented, the poet uses some techniques we often see on the screen. Look at this description of the knife-grinder:

> The sad, sharp-chinn'd old man, with worn clothes, and broad shoulder-band of leather;

In film, this is called a 'close-up'. The lens closes in on one person or object and we see them in fine detail.

1 Films use camera angles. Do you know about camera angles? Share your ideas or do some research if you are not sure of the meaning.

2 Then look at the next lines from the poem and discuss the questions below:

> Myself, effusing and fluid – a phantom curiously floating – now here absorb'd and arrested;

> The group, (an unminded point, set in a vast surrounding;)

- What do you notice about the 'camera angle'?
- What is the effect?
- What could the poet be attempting to do here?

HINT

Make notes in the way you find most useful – a mind map or perhaps bulleted points.

Make sure your handwriting is clear and easy to read so that you can refer to your notes easily.

EXERCISE 1.1

1   The poem 'Sparkles from the Wheel' is descriptive. Makes notes by answering these questions:
   ■   Which moments of description come to life in your imagination?
   ■   What sights or sounds are there?
   ■   What would it feel like to be part of the crowd?

2   The poet has divided the poem into four verses. Describe how the viewpoint of the poem changes from verse to verse.

3   Choose one of these two thoughts about the poem and write 4–5 sentences to build on it:
   ■   It doesn't **rhyme** but it does use other poetic effects.
   ■   The poet has chosen some strange words.

KEY WORDS

rhyme the endings of words that sound the same, usually at the ends of lines in a poem

colon (:) introduces something that is to follow

semi-colon (;) links two independent clauses and can be used between sentences that have a common theme to create a pause and emphasis effect, like the effect of a full stop

phrase a group of words that do not contain a verb, e.g. She ate her breakfast *while on the bus*.

rhythm the beat or pace (speed) of a poem. It is formed by the pattern of stressed and unstressed words.

Key skills

Punctuation in poetry

Poets use dashes, commas, **colons** and **semi-colons** to organise information and to indicate to readers to pause in some places. If there is no punctuation at the end of a line in a poem, you don't need to pause.

Remember:
■   **colons** (:) introduce something that is to follow: a list of items, a speaker in a play or an idea.
■   **semi-colons** (;) link two independent clauses. The semi-colon can be replaced by a full stop.
■   **commas** (,) separate information or some clauses or items in a list.
■   **hyphens** (-) can be used to make compound words, including some numbers, with some prefixes. (Note: not all compound words have hyphens.)
■   **dashes** (–) are short horizontal lines that are placed in the middle of a line of text. We use dashes to give emphasis to a word or **phrase**. Dashes can also be used as a stylistic device, instead of commas or to give **rhythm** to a poem.

LET'S TALK

Look at the following lines from the poem 'Sparkles from the Wheel'. Discuss how the poet uses punctuation marks to add shades of meaning.

Myself, effusing and fluid – a phantom curiously floating – now here absorb'd and arrested;

The group, (an unminded point, set in a vast surrounding;)
The attentive, quiet children – the loud, proud, restive base of the streets;

■   Which punctuation marks make the reader stop and think?
■   Which punctuation marks are used to add information?
■   Why does the poet use brackets ( ) instead of a dash in the following line: *The group, (an unminded point, set in a vast surrounding;)*? What more does this tell us about the group?

OF CUTLERY

D & SET

Rhythm

Rhythm is the beat or pace (speed) of a poem. Some poems have a **regular** rhythm which is formed by using a pattern of stressed and unstressed words and syllables.

Other poems have an **irregular** rhythm which is closely related to the rhythm of natural speech. The poet may use short and long sentences as well as punctuation such as dashes. This creates an irregular rhythm which gives emphasis to certain words and ideas.

EXERCISE 1.2

Write a response to this comment about the poem:

'The rhythm is irregular. There are lots of pauses in the middle of lines with dashes and semi-colons. Why?'

Reflection

A poem is never understood straight away. Even experienced poets feel confused or lost when they read a poem. To understand a poem, you need to describe your journey of understanding. These questions will help you to describe your journey.

- What were your first thoughts?
- What words or phrases confused you?
- What has helped you understand a little more?
- Are there any questions you still have?

Reading

Building on poetry to describe a scene

You are going to read another descriptive poem. This time the scene is in Jamaica.

> **HINT**
> Remember that you do not need to understand everything all at once. It takes time and imagination. Find an image or a phrase that opens the door a little and take a few steps through. Start by finding one thing you *do* understand from the poem, however small, and work from there.

Poet: A.L. Hendriks

Arthur Lemière Hendriks was a Jamaican poet and writer (1922-92). He became well known as a television broadcaster and director in Jamaica.

KEY WORD

enjambment the continuation of a sentence into the next line of a poem

'Road to Lacovia'

This is a long, forbidding road, a narrow,
hard aisle of asphalt under
a high gothic arch of bamboos.
Along it a woman drags a
makeshift barrow
in slanting rain, and thunder:
a thin woman who wears no shoes.

This is St Elizabeth, a hard parish
to work; but when you are born
on land, you want to work that land.
Nightfall comes here swift and harsh and deep, but garish
flames of lightning show up torn
cheap clothing barely patched, and

a face patterned by living. Every sharp line
of this etching has the mark
of struggle. To the eye, unyielding
bleak earth has brought her close to famine;
yet through this wild descent of dark
this woman dares to walk, and sing.

A.L. Hendriks

Activity 1.3

1 In a small group, read the poem aloud, taking it in turns to read a few lines each.
2 After reading the poem discuss what you think the poet is saying. For example, what is his attitude to his subject – is he just describing the village and the scenery, or does the poem carry a deeper meaning?
3 Consider his choice of words and how they convey the impression of the surroundings. Finally, think about what is being suggested by the poem's last sentence ('To the eye ... dares to walk, and sing').
4 Read the poem aloud again and discuss the rhythm of the poem. How does this add to the description? Does the punctuation have a special effect? What other poetic devices does the poet use? Think about enjambment.
5 Does the poet use rhyme? Can you see a pattern in any rhyming words?

Writing

Editing and improving a written response to a poem

EXERCISE 1.3

A student has written a response to the poem below. Your task is to rewrite one of the paragraphs to add more detail and depth. Think about the teacher's comments in the margin and add more depth. If you do not agree with the response, you can change it to your opinions.

> Good, but will you make it clear why you like it?

> What does the description of the woman and her barrow suggest about the life she leads?

> How does the poem describe the lightning? What is suggested by the word 'garish'? You could also comment more about what it reveals about her clothing. The rain is also described as 'slanting' in the first verse – it would be a good idea to refer to that in your comment as well.

> Again, you have referred to the poet's choice of words without really developing any of your comments. It would help to explain how these words reinforce the picture of the woman's life.

I like this poem. It makes you think about the hard lives of people who live in country areas. It describes a woman pulling a 'makeshift barrow' along a long, narrow road. It is raining hard and the woman, who is thin, is not wearing shoes.

In the second verse, the poem tells us that the scene is in St Elizabeth, an area of Jamaica. Lacovia is a town in the parish of St Elizabeth. The poet describes it as 'a hard parish to work'. It isn't clear if this means that work is hard in the area or that it is hard to find work there — perhaps it has both meanings. It also says that if you are born on this land, then you want to work that land. The last three lines of this verse (and the beginning of the next) tell us that nightfall comes quickly here and there also seems to be a thunderstorm as it says that the lightning shows us the woman's face which has been 'patterned by living' and the cheap clothing that she is wearing.

In the last verse, the poet repeats that the woman's life is hard, and that she is 'close to famine', which means that she can't have much to eat. However, she is singing as she walks and this would seem to suggest that she is happy, though I'm not sure why.

The poem consists of three verses of six lines each and in each verse the words rhyme (line 1 with line 4, line 2 with line 5 and line 3 with line 6). Many of the words in the poem remind us of the harsh life the woman lives ('forbidding', 'hard', 'harsh', 'bleak', 'struggle', 'cheap', 'famine'). The poem also talks about the cruel weather and how the 'garish … lightning' shows up the woman's cheap, patched clothes and the lines 'etched' on her face.

> Good point, but it would help if you explored further the implications of the two meanings.

> You need to ask yourself 'Why?' and then explain your answer as this last line contains the poem's main message. Try to explain fully the meaning of this last sentence, starting from 'To the eye, unyielding bleak earth …'. What does it tell us about the woman's spirit?

> Rather than describing the way the poem rhymes, try to comment on the effect. Does the rhyme emphasise certain key words in the poem?

> What is 'etching'? Why is this choice of word particularly apt here?

Speaking

Performing a poem

Poetry began before writing – poems are meant to be spoken aloud. The patterns of rhythm, rhyme and letter sounds are for the ear. In this task you will develop a performance of a poem, thinking about how to connect the sound and meaning of the poem.

You are going to read another descriptive poem. This one is by Robert Frost, whom you may remember from Stage 7.

Robert Frost made this poem from simple, everyday language. When you hear the poem spoken, you could believe you are listening to the conversation of a friend or relative, telling you about their day.

Poet:

Robert Frost

Robert Lee Frost was an American poet (1874-1963). He is much admired for his descriptions of rural life.

WORD ATTACK SKILLS

Work out what the following words mean from the context of the lines in which they appear:

✔ diverged
✔ trodden
✔ hence

'The Road Not Taken'

Two roads **diverged** in a yellow wood,
And sorry I could not travel both
And be one traveler, long I stood
And looked down one as far as I could
To where it bent in the undergrowth;

Then took the other, as just as fair,
And having perhaps the better claim,
Because it was grassy and wanted wear;
Though as for that the passing there
Had worn them really about the same,

And both that morning equally lay
In leaves no step had **trodden** black.
Oh, I kept the first for another day!
Yet knowing how way leads on to way,
I doubted if I should ever come back.

I shall be telling this with a sigh
Somewhere ages and ages **hence**:
Two roads diverged in a wood, and I –
I took the one less traveled by,
And that has made all the difference.

Robert Frost

Spelling

Robert Frost uses the American spelling of the words 'traveler' and 'traveled'. In British English we usually double the final 'l' when we add a suffix (that starts with a vowel) to a word with more than one syllable. Check in a dictionary if you are not sure of a spelling.

LET'S TALK

Read the poem 'The Road Not Taken' together, and discuss the ideas in the speech bubbles.

1   What meaning or meanings can you find in the poem? Is it simply about a walk in the woods, told as a poem?
2   Is there another way to understand what Robert Frost says? Would it be a better poem if it used more 'poetic' language?

> Can simple, everyday language be poetic?

> Does simple language mean this is a simple poem?

> If the language is simple, the meaning is simple.

Key skills

Developing a performance

Lines

Read through the poem. Look out for enjambment and **caesura**. Some lines may end in the middle of a sentence. Try reading these lines with a pause at the end, and try reading them without a pause, running one line on to the next.

Which do you think helps you to understand the poem better?

Should you always pause, or always run on, or make a choice in each case?

Patterns

A poem is held together because words and sounds are linked through pattern. When you say a poem aloud, patterns can help the **audience** understand how the meaning fits together across lines and verses.

Look for:
- the pattern of rhymes
- **repetition** of consonant sounds (**alliteration** and **sibilance**)
- repetition of vowel sounds (**assonance**).

How could these sounds be related to the meaning of the poem? Do they enhance the meaning?

Rhythm

The rhythm of a poem is important for performance:

- Where are the pauses? Some pauses will be shown using punctuation. Other pauses may come from the meaning of the sentence.
- Do any lines hurry or skip along the rhythm of the words? Do any lines move more slowly?
- How could these rhythms be related to the meaning of the poem?

Performance

> I find it embarrassing to perform on my own in front of the class.

> I will try to learn a verse off by heart – it is easier to perform if you know your lines.

> I will need to have some notes to help my memory.

> I keep making a mistake in the same place.

> The final line seems important – but I'm not sure if it's a happy or sad ending.

Discuss the challenges that face you. How can you enhance your performance?

Audience

For whom are you performing? What will get their attention? Decide the best way to present this as a performance. Do you need anything for support? For example, a print-out of the poem in large print or some visual prompts such as an image or quotations to focus the audience's attention.

EXERCISE 1.4

As you listen to other groups' performances of the poem, make notes on anything you spot that is interesting. What do you notice about how other groups have decided to perform the poem? Think about rhythm, sound patterns, meaning and confidence.

1 Write one sentence to praise a decision. Give a reason.

2 Write one sentence to offer advice for how to improve. Give a reason.

Activity 1.4

In a group, try reading 'The Road Not Taken' aloud between you, paying attention to different elements that would enhance your performance of the poem. Think about what you are trying to convey at different points in the poem and why. Make sure everybody gets a chance to perform part of the poem and then perform it as a group to the class.

Author:

H.G. Wells

H.G. Wells (1866 1946) was a British author, journalist and historian who is best known for his science-fiction **novels** such as *The Time Machine* and *The War of the Worlds*.

Reading

Science fiction

Science fiction is a **genre** in which writers bring imaginary worlds to life, in the future or in different places. Writers often explore the use of technology and its impact on societies and the resulting social changes.

At the end of H.G. Wells's classic science-fiction story *The Time Machine*, the Time Traveller takes his machine millions of years into the future until he stops at a point when it seems as if the end of the world is soon to take place.

Extract: *The Time Machine*

Far away up the desolate slope I heard a harsh scream, and saw a thing like a huge white butterfly go slanting and fluttering up into the sky and, circling, disappear over some low hillocks beyond. The sound of its voice was so dismal that I shivered and seated myself more firmly upon the machine. Looking round me again, I saw that, quite near, what I had taken to be a reddish mass of rock was moving slowly towards me. Then I saw the thing was really a monstrous crab-like creature. Can you imagine a crab as large as **yonder** table, with its many legs moving slowly and uncertainly, its big claws swaying, its long antennae, like **carters' whips**, waving and feeling, and its **stalked** eyes gleaming at you on either side of its metallic front? Its back was **corrugated** and ornamented with ungainly **bosses**, and a greenish **incrustation** blotched it here and there. I could see the many **palps** of its complicated mouth flickering and feeling as it moved.

As I stared at this sinister apparition crawling towards me, I felt a tickling on my cheek as though a fly had lighted there. I tried to brush it away with my hand, but in a moment it returned, and almost immediately came another by my ear. I struck at this and caught something threadlike. It was drawn swiftly out of my hand. With a frightful **qualm**, I turned, and I saw that I had grasped the antenna of another monster crab that stood just behind me. Its evil eyes were wriggling on their stalks, its mouth was all alive with appetite, and its vast ungainly claws, smeared with an **algal** slime, were descending upon me. In a moment my hand was on the lever, and I had placed a month between myself and these monsters. But I was still on the same beach, and I saw them distinctly now as soon as I stopped. Dozens of them seemed to be crawling here and there, in the **sombre** light, among the **foliated** sheets of intense green.

I cannot convey the sense of abominable desolation that hung over the world. The red eastern sky, the northward blackness, the salt Dead Sea, the

WORD ATTACK SKILLS

Work out the meaning of the following words from the context of the lines in which they appear:

- ✔ yonder
- ✔ stalked
- ✔ corrugated
- ✔ bosses
- ✔ incrustation
- ✔ palps
- ✔ sombre
- ✔ darkling
- ✔ eddying
- ✔ sable

Spotlight on: science fiction

Common elements in science-fiction writing include:

- ■ imaginary worlds
- ■ time travel and teleportation
- ■ extra-terrestrial lifeforms
- ■ space travel and space exploration
- ■ interplanetary warfare.

stony beach crawling with these foul, slow-stirring monsters, the uniform poisonous-looking green of the lichenous plants, the thin air that hurts one's lungs; all contributed to an appalling effect. I moved on a hundred years, and there was the same red sun – a little larger, a little duller – the same dying sea, the same chill air, and the same crowd of earthy crustacea creeping in and out among the green weed and the red rocks. And in the westward sky I saw a curved pale line like a vast new moon.

So I travelled, stopping ever and again, in great strides of a thousand years or more, drawn on by the mystery of the earth's fate, watching with a strange fascination the sun grow larger and duller in the westward sky, and the life of the old earth ebb away. At last, more than thirty million years hence, the huge red-hot dome of the sun had come to obscure nearly a tenth part of the darkling heavens. Then I stopped once more, for the crawling multitude of crabs had disappeared, and the red beach, save for its livid green liverworts and lichens, seemed lifeless. And now it was flecked with white. A bitter cold assailed me. Rare white flakes ever and again came eddying down. To the north-eastward, the glare of snow lay under the starlight of the sable sky, and I could see an undulating crest of hillocks pinkish white. There were fringes of ice along the sea margin, with drifting masses further out; but the main expanse of that salt ocean, all bloody under the eternal sunset, was still unfrozen.

H.G. Wells

EXERCISE 1.5

1 Describe, using your own words, the appearance of the monstrous crab mentioned in the first paragraph.

2 Which two words in the second paragraph describe the Time Traveller's fearful reaction to realising that he was being attacked by the second crab's antenna?

3 How did the Time Traveller escape from the crabs?

4 How many years into the future had the Time Traveller travelled by the end of his journey?

EXERCISE 1.6

Think about the language the writer uses in this story.

1 In the first three paragraphs, the narrator describes the 'abominable desolation' of the world of the distant future. Explain what you think is meant by this phrase.

2 By looking closely at the words the writer uses to describe the landscape and the creatures that are part of it, explain how he creates this atmosphere.

LET'S TALK

Do you prefer stories about the real world or imagined worlds? Can you begin to explain why?

Spotlight on: atmosphere

A writer creates atmosphere in a scene by describing a place in a way that brings the place to life. The writer might describe not only the details, but also the emotions of the people in it.

KEY WORDS

atmosphere how the physical situation or environment feels
setting the place or places in which the events occur

Activity 1.5

H.G. Wells has the job of describing a very unusual world. Isn't it incredible to think that just a few squiggles on a page can describe a world of the far future?

Work in a group. Imagine a film of this story.
- What scenery would you use?
- What lighting effects would you use?
- How could you show the great jumps through time?

Discuss how you could use these ideas to bring it to life on the screen.

Activity 1.6

Still working in a group, compare the extract from *The Time Machine* with another science-fiction story that you know. Look at the 'Spotlight on: science fiction' box for ideas.
- Does the other story also describe an unusual world? What is unusual in the other text?
- Does the other story also include time travel?
- Why do you think stories like this are popular?
- Why might readers choose science-fiction texts over non-fiction texts such as historical accounts or travel writing?

Creating an atmosphere

Have you ever been in a place that creates a strong **atmosphere**? Have you 'felt' strong emotions coming from your surroundings – maybe a particular building or room, or perhaps an outdoor **setting**?

Read the extracts from the stories and novels over the next few pages. Each extract brings a particular place to life, with language that is used carefully to create an atmosphere.

Author: Alexander McCall Smith

Alexander McCall Smith (born 1948) has written more than 100 academic books, short stories and children's stories. The extract on the right is from *In the Company of Cheerful Ladies* which is part of a series of novels that feature the character Mma Precious Ramotswe. The stories are set in Botswana.

WORD ATTACK SKILLS

Work out the meaning of the following words from the context of the story:

- ✔ bents
- ✔ foliage
- ✔ landlocked
- ✔ dispute
- ✔ witnessed
- ✔ incredulously

Extract: *In the Company of Cheerful Ladies*

Mma Ramotswe was sitting alone in her favourite café, on the edge of the shopping centre at the Gaborone end of Tlokweng Road. It was a Saturday, the day she preferred above all others, a day on which one might do as much or as little as one liked, a day to have lunch with a friend at the President Hotel, or, as on that day, to sit by oneself and think about the **bents** of the week, and the state of the world. This café was a good place to be, for several reasons. Firstly, there was the view, that of a stand of eucalyptus trees with **foliage** of comforting dark green which made a sound like the sea when the wind blew through the leaves. Or that, at least, was the sound which Mma Ramotswe imagined the sea to make. She had never seen the ocean, which was far away from **landlocked** Botswana; far away across the deserts of Namibia, across the red sands and dry mountains. But she could imagine it when she listened to the eucalyptus trees in the wind and closed her eyes. Perhaps one day she would see it, and would stand on the shore and let the waves wash over her feet. Perhaps.

The other advantage that this café had was the fact that the tables were out on an open verandah, and there was always something to watch. That morning, for instance, she had seen a minor **dispute** between a teenage girl and her boyfriend – an exchange of words that she did not catch but which was clear enough in its meaning – and she had **witnessed** a woman scrape the side of a neighbouring car while she tried to park. The woman had stopped, quickly inspected the damage, and had then driven off. Mma Ramotswe had watched this **incredulously**, and had half-risen to her feet to protest, but was too late: the woman's car had by then turned the corner and disappeared and she did not even have time to see its number-plate.

She had sat down again and poured herself another cup of tea. It was not true that such a thing could not have happened in the old Botswana – it could – but it was undoubtedly true that this was much more likely to happen today. There were many selfish people about these days, people who seemed not to care if they scraped the cars of others or bumped into people while walking on the street.

Alexander McCall Smith

LET'S TALK

Work in a pair. Find words in the extract that bring the scene to life and set the atmosphere. Share your ideas with other learners.

EXERCISE 1.7

Imagine you are sitting in a café near where you live. Write a paragraph to describe what you see, hear and feel.

Key skills

Compound and complex sentences

Writers use **complex** and **compound sentences** to add detail to what they are writing and to create effects. Look at these examples from the extracts.

In this sentence the author creates the effect of moving along by adding phrases and **clauses** and using commas to connect the clauses:

> So I travelled, stopping ever and again, in great strides of a thousand years or more, drawn on by the mystery of the earth's fate, watching with a strange fascination the sun grow larger and duller in the westward sky, and the life of the old earth ebb away.

In this sentence the author sets the scene by using a series of clauses to create an emotion or feeling about a day:

> It was a Saturday, the day she preferred above all others, a day on which one might do as much or as little as one liked, a day to have lunch with a friend at the President Hotel, or, as on that day, to sit by oneself and think about the bents of the week, and the state of the world.

In this sentence the author creates an effect of suspense with different clauses and punctuation:

> Mma Ramotswe had watched this incredulously, and had half-risen to her feet to protest, but was too late: the woman's car had by then turned the corner and disappeared and she did not even have time to see its number-plate.

Remember: clauses can be joined by **connectives**, commas, colons or semi-colons or dashes. Compound sentences are often joined by connectives such as *and, or, but,* or *so*.

KEY WORDS

complex sentence a long sentence that contains one main (independent) and at least one dependent (or subordinate) clause. A subordinate clause does not make sense on its own.

compound sentence a sentence consisting of two or more main (independent) clauses that are linked in some way

clause a group of words containing a **verb**. A main clause makes sense on its own; a subordinate clause depends on a main clause for its sense to be clear.

connective any word such as a conjunction, preposition or **adverb** that connects one clause to another

verb a word that expresses an action or a state of being, e.g. Joe *ate* his dinner. Joe no longer *felt* hungry

adverb a word, frequently ending in *-ly*, that is used to describe the action expressed by a verb, e.g. Joe ate *hungrily*.

Activity 1.7

Work in a pair. Look at the compound and complex sentences below, which are from the extracts you have read. Find the clauses by identifying the verbs. Then discuss how the clauses are linked and what effect each sentence has.

1 I tried to brush it away with my hand, but in a moment it returned, and almost immediately came another by my ear.

2 The woman had stopped, quickly inspected the damage, and had then driven off.

3 She had never seen the ocean, which was far away from landlocked Botswana; far away across the deserts of Namibia, across the red sands and dry mountains. But she could imagine it when she listened to the eucalyptus trees in the wind and closed her eyes. Perhaps one day she would see it, and would stand on the shore and let the waves wash over her feet.

Activity 1.8

Add details and effects to the following sentences by adding at least two more clauses to each sentence. Use commas, dashes or semi-colons to link the clauses. Then share your sentences with others in a group.

1 It was Sunday and I had nothing to do.
2 He stopped where the roads diverged.

Here is an extract from a short story by a Russian author, Yuri Nagibin, who tells how a young schoolteacher, Anna Vasilevna, learns an important lesson about the natural world. In this scene, the narrator is being led through the forest, in search of a particular tree.

Author:
Yuri Nagibin

Yuri Markovich Nagibin (Юрий Ма́ркович Наги́бин) was a Russian Soviet writer, screenwriter and novelist (1920–94).

WORD ATTACK SKILLS

These words are made up of two smaller words joined together. What do the smaller words mean? What could they mean when put together?

✔ snowdrift
✔ sun-dappled
✔ smoky-blue

Extract: 'The Winter Oak'

And the forest led them on still farther along its intricate, tangled paths. It seemed as if there was no end to the trees, the **snowdrifts** and the silence of the **sun-dappled** twilight.

Suddenly, in the distance, a **smoky-blue** chink appeared. The trees began to thin out, there was more space and it was fresher. Soon there was no longer a chink, but a broad shaft of sunlight appeared before them, and in it something glistened and sparkled, swarming with frosty stars.

The path went round a hazel bush, and straight away the forest fell away on either side. In the middle of the glade, clothed in glittering raiment, huge and majestic as a cathedral, stood an oak. It seemed as if the trees had respectfully stood aside to give their older brother room to display himself in all his strength. The lower branches spread out over the glade like a canopy.

Snow was packed into the deep corrugations of the bark, and the trunk, three times the normal girth, seemed to be embroidered with silver thread. Few of the leaves that had withered in the autumn had fallen, and the oak was covered right up to the top with leaves encased in snow.

'There it is, the winter oak!'

Yuri Nagibin

Key skills

Personification

Writers use the literary device of **personification** to give more vivid descriptions of things or ideas. They represent the things as people or as having human forms. This can help readers to connect with and understand the object that is personified, and can also evoke an emotional reaction in readers.

For example, in the sentence below, the author says that the oak tree is 'clothed' in 'raiment' (wearing clothes). This helps us to 'see' the tree and perhaps to admire it as something special, at which we can wonder.

> In the middle of the glade, clothed in glittering raiment, huge and majestic as a cathedral, stood an oak.

EXERCISE 1.8

1 Find two more examples of personification in the extract on page 17.

2 Explain how the writer has used personification to enhance the sense of magic or wonder in the forest.

LET'S TALK

Work in a pair. Read the following descriptive piece which is setting the scene for an important event. Discuss how the colours and descriptions set the **mood**. Is this optimistic or pessimistic?

Extract: 'Pink Lemonade and Cookies'

The lime-green patio umbrella flapped happily in the breeze. It covered strawberry slushies, watermelon pies, and bright cheerful stacks of donuts. Emily stepped outside to feature a crystal pitcher of pink lemonade and a spray of warm cookies in the center of the table. She had on her favourite dress and knew that, as soon as he stepped through the patio gate, her life would never be the same again.

Kit Kittelstad

EXERCISE 1.9

Write a paragraph using colours to set a scene. Choose to convey either an optimistic or a pessimistic atmosphere.

EXERCISE 1.10

The last three extracts have each described a distinct and specific setting. Which of them had the greatest effect on you? Which was the most effective at creating a sense of atmosphere? Explain your choice in a short paragraph, referring to the language used in the extract.

Writing

Creating an atmosphere

You have read and responded to a range of poetry and fiction. Each piece described a specific place, creating a sense of atmosphere for a human being in that scene.

- Some of the places were city or street scenes: Walt Whitman described a street scene, pausing to watch and bring to life a typical moment.
- Some of the places were woodland scenes: Robert Frost described a walk through the woods, pausing to decide which path to take.
- One piece was a totally imagined scene: H.G. Wells described a moment at the shore, millions of years into the future.

Now it is your turn. You will write a descriptive piece, with the goal of creating a strong sense of atmosphere.

EXERCISE 1.11

This is the planning phase.

Here are some prompts to begin thinking. You do not have to make a final decision now.

1 Think about each decision to be made. Draw on strong memories, or times when you have sensed the atmosphere of a place.

2 Use a mind map to plan your ideas. Make simple notes of possibilities.

3 Make your notes quickly, but make sure your writing is legible so that you can read it.

Activity 1.9

Now you have to make some decisions about your scene.

Work with a partner. Take it in turns to ask and answer these questions:

- Will you describe a real place or imagined world?
- Is it a street or city scene, or a natural setting?
- Who will be in your scene?
- What will they notice?
- What atmosphere will you create?

HINT

Getting started is often the trickiest stage. Once you've done this, it should get easier.

Vocabulary

Create a list of specific words that you could use to bring your scene to life. You could use a table like this:

Colours	Feelings	Sounds	Textures	Senses

Spotlight on: feedback

When you're reading someone's work, you need to respond sensitively. Don't just point out mistakes. Focus on what works well just as much as on what needs improving.

EXERCISE 1.12

1 Work alone and write a first draft. Just write without being critical. Get your ideas on paper. Try to use full and correct sentences, but focus for now on allowing the ideas to begin flowing.

2 Take a moment to read back through your first draft. You may decide you don't like parts of it. You may notice that some sentences are not fully accurate. Don't worry. You can change anything at this second stage.

Activity 1.10

Now you will take your writing and develop it.

Work with a partner. Read each other's first drafts, and discuss these points:

- **Atmosphere** What atmosphere were you aiming for? Which parts achieve this? Where could it be improved? Have you tried to use personification?

- **Vocabulary** Which word choices are effective and bring the scene to life? Have you focused on one sense more than others?
- **Narrator** Who is in your scene? Is it clear to the reader? Does the viewpoint move around the scene?
- **Sentences** Have you used short and long (complex or compound) sentences and different punctuation to create different effects?

EXTENSION

You could also think about the film techniques you could use to help your writing:

- **Close-ups** What could you zoom in on and describe in great detail? How will this relate to the atmosphere you will create?
- **Movement and long-shots** Will you even see the whole scene? How will your gaze or narrator move through the scene?
- **Lighting effects** How will colours and the sky enhance your sense of atmosphere?

Key skills

Editing

Your sentences need to be accurate in order to have the desired impact on your reader. Here are some things to think about:

- **Punctuation** Does it help the reader to understand the text? Would it be more effective to change it? Have you overused some punctuation marks?
- **Verb tense** Does the tense help to set the scene?
- **Spelling** Make sure you have spelled words correctly.

Reviewing

Reflect on your learning in this chapter.

Reading

- Which of the texts did you prefer?
- Would you read any of the texts again, or read more from that author?
- Write a list of the skills and techniques you learned from one or more of these authors.
- How do you feel about poetry now?
- Has your confidence or opinion about poetry changed since you began this unit?

Speaking and listening

- Performing a poem can be a daunting task. How did you approach this?
- Did you memorise some of the lines?
- How did it feel to share your writing or ideas with a group or a partner?
- Did it help to work with others when planning your own writing or responses?
- Do you think you worked well as part of a small group or with a partner? What do you think you could improve?

Writing

- What techniques did you use in your own writing?
- What did you change between your first and second drafts? How did you decide what to change?
- What stage of the writing process do you enjoy? What do you need to work on more?

Key skills

- What vocabulary have you learned?
- List five new words you have learned.

If you enjoyed reading these extracts, you might enjoy:
- *Divergent* by Veronica Roth
- *The Girl of Ink and Stars* by Kiran Millwood Hargrave
- *The Haven* by Simon Lelic
- *Run, Rebel* by Manjeet Mann
- *Poems Aloud: An anthology of poems to read out loud* by Joseph Coelho
- *A Poem for Every Night of the Year* edited by Allie Esiri

Reading
★ Historical text from different cultures
★ A 17th-century diary
★ A 20th-century diary

Speaking and listening
★ A group discussion about personal expression
★ A debate about social media and digital communication
★ Expressing your thoughts and feelings through language

EXPRESS YOURSELF

Writing
★ A balanced report on celebrity influencers
★ Editing and improving your work

Key skills
★ Analysing language more deeply
★ Identifying formal and informal language
★ Planning a diary entry
★ Punctuation in diaries: dashes and commas
★ Using a graphic organiser

LET'S TALK

There are many ways to express your personality, feelings and opinions. Some people use one or more of the following:

■ writing, such as poetry, a diary, or a blog

■ music: playing or creating songs and tunes

■ art, such as painting, dancing or drama.

Can you think of any other forms of self-expression?

How do you like to express yourself? What would you like to try?

Speaking and listening

Personal expression

People have different ways of expressing their thoughts and feelings.

> If anything's bothering me, I always talk to my sister. She's a really good listener. I normally feel better just saying my worries out loud.

> I have so many ideas in my head. That's why I started a **blog**, so I could share them with anyone and everyone.

> I write a **diary**. I wouldn't want anyone to read it, but I like to remember the ups and downs.

> I want to be a **vlogger** when I am older, so I practise in front of the mirror.

> My **journal** is full of funny memories. I let all my family and friends read it to cheer them up.

Activity 2.1

Work in a small group.

Discuss these prompts. Your group may agree or disagree, but you should make sure to respect different opinions, and listen with an open mind.

- It is important to have a way to express your thoughts and feelings.
- There is a wrong way to express yourself.
- Some people won't let anyone read their diary.
- It is best to keep your opinions to yourself.
- Most people are not good listeners.
- You can learn by listening to another person's opinion.

Expression and social media

The internet has generated new ways to communicate and spread opinions and knowledge.

Influencers and celebrities use blogs, vlogs and social media to spread their influence in different areas, including:

- fashion
- food and cooking
- shopping
- travel
- tackling discrimination
- environmental issues.

What do you think about the power of the internet? Do you think it is a positive or a negative way to communicate?

Spend a moment jotting down your thoughts about this topic.

My opinions of the internet as a communication tool are …

Activity 2.2

Do you think the internet is a positive or a negative way to communicate?

1   Hold a debate on this issue as a class or in a small group.
    Share your ideas and respond to each other.

2   As you listen, make notes in a table like the one below:

Positive aspects	Negative aspects	Neutral aspects

Choose the most appropriate way to take notes. Remember, you need to engage with the discussion as you write so choose quick and efficient ways such as bullet points, key words or abbreviations.

3   Work in a pair. Work through each column in the table to summarise and evaluate the discussion.

What were the main opinions?

What did you strongly agree or disagree with?

Have any of your opinions changed?

Did you find it easy to listen?

Did you feel confident to share your own opinions?

How would you improve the discussion?

Spotlight on: a successful debate

- Some people may have strong feelings.
- Some people may disagree and want to speak out against each other.

Agree a set of rules as a class to enable everyone to feel respected, and to have their opinions fairly considered.

Writing

Choosing connectives to write a balanced report

Social media has allowed many people to become 'influencers'.

Influencers use their online following to share their opinions or ideas, and sometimes to advertise products. Some people become famous in this way.

Activity 2.3

1   Here are some students' responses to Asahi's post. Discuss these responses. What do they have in common? How can points of disagreement be useful?

> Despite her sweet introduction, I would rather trust a qualified professional than an influencer.

> On one hand I would ignore her advice, because she has not studied properly. On the other hand, I do appreciate the idea of getting inspiration from nature.

> You could argue that it is pointless, as so many people post videos like these. In contrast, it is positive to be able to share ideas with people from all over the world.

> Although she is not fully qualified, she may have a natural talent.

Asahi Sasaki   FOLLOW

♡ ◯ ✈   🔖

♥ 508 likes

Hello, I'm Asahi Sasaki from Japan.
I make video tutorials about how to do makeup, fashion, hair and nails :)
I have never studied at a beauty school. I learned mainly from gurus on YouTube and in fashion magazines.
I get inspiration from fashionable Japanese women and little things around me. For example, flowers blooming in the garden or packages of sweets …

2   Discuss how these phrases allow the responders to describe positive and negative aspects of their response.
   ▪ Despite …, …
   ▪ On the one hand, … On the other hand, …
   ▪ You could argue that … In contrast, you might think …
   ▪ Although …, it is possible that …

3   Use one of these phrases to write a balanced summary of your debate about communication via the internet.

4   Now use a combination of these phrases to write a balanced response paragraph to the idea of celebrity influencers, using these sentence structures to develop and link your ideas. Try to show two sides of the argument.

Reading

Preparing to read a variety of texts

Before the internet, many people kept diaries, and some still write in a diary today. They are often private or secret diaries.

A person writing a diary may not expect or want anyone else to read it.

> **LET'S TALK**
>
> Before you read the diary extract on page 28, discuss these questions with a partner:
> - Why do you think some people write a diary, if no one will read it?
> - What would you do if you found someone's diary?

The following extracts are from the diary kept by a young Dutch girl, Anne Frank, who lived in hiding with her family in Amsterdam during the Second World War.

Anne's diary (which she called 'Kitty') includes details of Anne's life and reveals the thoughts and feelings of an extraordinary schoolgirl.

This diary was never intended for publication, but it has become very famous since it was found and published.

Read the extract carefully and then answer the questions.

Extract: *The Diary of a Young Girl* (1)

Monday, 26 July 1943

Dearest Kitty,

Yesterday was a very **tumultuous** day, and we're still all **wound up**. Actually, you may wonder if there's ever a day that passes without some kind of excitement.

The first warning siren went off in the morning while we were at breakfast, but we paid no attention, because it only meant that the planes were crossing the coast. I had a terrible headache, so I lay down for an hour after breakfast and then went to the office at about two. At two-thirty Margot had finished her office work and was just gathering her things together when the sirens began wailing again. So she and I trooped back upstairs. None too soon, it seems, for less than five minutes later the guns were booming so loudly that we went and stood in the passage. The house shook and the bombs kept falling. I was clutching my 'escape bag', more because I wanted to have something to hold on to than because I wanted to run away. I know we can't leave here, but if we had to, being seen on the streets would be just as dangerous as getting caught in an air raid. After half an hour the drone of engines **faded** and the house began to hum with activity again. Peter emerged from his lookout post in the front attic, Dussel remained in the front office, Mrs van D. felt safest in the private office, Mr van Daan had been watching from the loft, and those of us on the landing spread out to watch the columns of smoke rising from the harbour. Before long the smell of fire was everywhere, and outside it looked as if the city were enveloped in a thick fog.

WORD ATTACK SKILLS

Use your word attack skills to work out the meaning of these words by using the surrounding words:

✔ tumultuous
✔ wound up
✔ faded

EXERCISE 2.1

Write a short paragraph giving your first impression of this text.
■ What do you think is happening?
■ What kind of person is Anne?
■ Would you be interested in reading more of this book? Why?

KEY WORDS

simile a figure of speech in which two things that are not obviously like each other are compared to make a description more vivid. A simile will often begin with a phrase introduced by 'like' or 'as', e.g. *The smoke hung from the chimney like a drooping flag.*

litotes a deliberate understatement which is made to give emphasis

EXERCISE 2.2

Answer these questions, using evidence from the text.

1 Peter 'emerged' from his lookout post. Explain fully the choice of this word.

2 What is the effect of this descriptive **simile**: 'as if the city were enveloped in a thick fog'?

3 Explain in your own words Anne's comment about her 'escape bag'. Why is the choice of word 'clutching' important here?

4 By referring to the extract from Anne Frank's diary, explain as fully as you can what you have learned about her character and the situation she was in.

LET'S TALK

Anne refers to her diary as 'Kitty' and she begins her entries:

Dear Kitty, ...

Use these prompts to discuss this idea.

■ Kitty is not a real person. Why would Anne write to an imaginary person?

■ What is different about writing a letter and writing a diary?

EXERCISE 2.3

Write a reply to Anne, from Kitty, as if Kitty were a real person.

Dear Anne,

...

Key skills

Analysing language more deeply

Here is how Anne goes on to describe her feelings about the fire.

'A big fire like that is not a pleasant sight'

This is an example of a technique called litotes (pronounced ly-toe-tees).

Litotes is a way of describing something by saying what it is *not*.

Here are some more examples from conversations:

HINT

Find some more examples of litotes. Collect and record them for use in your own writing.

EXTENSION

Find out more about the life of Anne Frank, and the circumstances in which she wrote her diary.

How are you feeling?

Not bad, thanks.

Sorry, but I will be late.

I'm not surprised.

Do you think you can fix this?

Well, it's not impossible.

Writing

Emotive language

A diary can be a powerful form of self-expression to:

- convey strong feelings
- describe hopes and dreams
- think deeply about life's issues.

WORD ATTACK SKILLS

List all the emotive words Anne uses in this extract.

Sort them into positive and negative categories.

KEY WORD

personality what a person's character and behaviour are like

Spotlight on: cultural context

A text can hold significant importance and meaning within a certain culture. 'Culture' refers to a particular way of life, including the customs and traditions, beliefs, knowledge and behaviours of a particular group of people at a particular time.

Extract: *The Diary of a Young Girl* (2)

It's utterly impossible for me to build my life on a foundation of chaos, suffering and death. I see the world being slowly transformed into a wilderness, I hear the approaching thunder that, one day, will destroy us too, I feel the suffering of millions. And yet, when I look up at the sky, I somehow feel that everything will change for the better, that this cruelty too will end, that peace and tranquillity will return once more. In the meantime, I must hold on to my ideals. Perhaps the day will come when I'll be able to realise them!

EXERCISE 2.4

1 What does this passage show about Anne's **personality**? Use evidence from the extract to support your interpretation.

2 Anne says: 'I must hold on to my ideals.'

Write a passage to describe your ideals and hopes for the future.

Use a balance of emotional language to explore your viewpoint fully.

I must hold on to my ideals, which means …

LET'S TALK

Many readers have found Anne's diary truly inspirational, especially considering that it was written by a teenager in such difficult circumstances.

What have you read or seen that inspires you? What texts or films have caused you to admire an individual?

Are there any texts that you consider important to your culture?

Key skills

Historical records

Diaries can be an important record of historical events.

They provide 'first-person accounts' or 'primary sources', which are written by people who witnessed an event themselves. Such sources are vital for modern historians.

The extract below describes the Great Fire of London in 1666. It was written by an eye-witness who saw and experienced the event himself: the seventeenth-century writer Samuel Pepys (pronounced peeps). Pepys was a quite important civil servant who lived in London at the time of King Charles II.

EXERCISE 2.5
Research the Great Fire of London in 1666 and write a short explanation of its historical significance.

WORD ATTACK SKILLS

Scan the text for unusual spellings or phrases that indicate this was written over 350 years ago. Make a list of all the unusual spellings.

Extract: *Samuel Pepys's Diary* (1)

September 2nd 1666 (Lord's day). Some of our mayds sitting up late last night to get things ready against [in preparation for] our feast to-day, Jane called us up about three in the morning, to tell us of a great fire they saw in the City. So I rose and slipped on my nightgowne, and went to her window, and thought it to be on the backside of Marke-lane at the farthest; but, being unused to such fires as followed, I thought it far enough off; and so went to bed again and to sleep.

Using formal and informal registers

Samuel Pepys did not write to impress anyone or to sound educated.

He wrote his diary in a form of code and had no intention that it would ever be published. However, after his death, his diaries were found and translated. They give us not just a unique insight into some of the great historical events of the time, but also an intimate understanding of the thoughts and attitudes of an individual human who was alive 350 years ago.

Activity 2.4

1 Now read the next passage.
   Work with a partner to make sense of the passage. Discuss possible interpretations. Do not worry if you make mistakes or seem confused at first – this is common when interpreting older texts.
   Samuel Pepys describes how he begins to realise just how serious the fire could be.

> About seven rose again to dress myself, and there looked out at the window, and saw the fire not so much as it was and further off … By and by Jane comes and tells me that she hears that above 300 houses have been burned down to-night by the fire we saw, and that it is now burning down all Fish-street, by London Bridge. So I made myself ready presently, and walked to the Tower [of London], and there got up upon one of the high places, Sir J. Robinson's little son going up with me; and there I did see the houses at that end of the bridge all on fire, and an infinite great fire on this and the other side the end of the bridge; which, among other people, did trouble me for poor little Michell and our Sarah on the bridge.

2 Rewrite the passage in modern English, as if describing the event in your own diary or in a letter to a friend, using informal or non-standard English.
   Your 'translation' should describe all of the details, but in a personal style, suited to a personal diary.
3 Evaluate your own approach to reading and interpreting texts. Use these prompts to help:
   - Do you ever lose concentration and find you have to re-read a sentence or paragraph?
   - What do you do if you meet an unfamiliar word?
   - What strategies do you use when you are confused by a text?
   - When do you feel successful as a reader? What helps you feel confident with difficult texts?
   - What advice would you give to someone who did not feel confident?

HINT
The language may seem unfamiliar and difficult on first reading, because it is in an old-fashioned style.

Reading

Comprehension and comparison

Here, Samuel Pepys goes on to describe the scene in great detail.

Read this extract and try to picture the scene in your imagination, then answer the questions on the next page.

Can you imagine how this would be filmed for news footage in modern times?

Extract: *Samuel Pepys's Diary* (2)

So down, with my heart full of trouble, to the Lieutenant of the Tower, who tells me that it begun this morning in the King's baker's house in Pudding-lane, and that it hath burned St Magnus's Church and most part of Fish-street already.

Everybody endeavouring to remove their goods, and flinging into the river or bringing them into lighters that layoff; poor people staying in their houses as long as till the very fire touched them, and then running into boats, or clambering from one pair of stairs by the water-side to another. And among other things, the poor pigeons, I perceive, were loth to leave their houses, but hovered about the windows and balconys till they were, some of them burned, their wings, and fell down.

…

Having staid, and in an hour's time seen the fire rage every way, and nobody, to my sight, endeavouring to quench it, but to remove their goods, and leave all to the fire, and having seen it get as far as the Steele-yard, and the wind mighty high and driving it into the City; and every thing, after so long a drought, proving combustible, even the very stones of churches

…

So I was called for, and did tell the King and Duke of Yorke what I saw, and that unless his Majesty did command houses to be pulled down nothing could stop the fire.

They seemed much troubled, and the King commanded me to go to my Lord Mayor from him, and command him to spare no houses, but to pull down before the fire every way.

EXERCISE 2.6

1 Where did Samuel Pepys think that the fire had begun and who told him it had started?

2 What were most people doing instead of trying to put out the fire?

3 What two things does Pepys say were making the fire worse?

4 What did Pepys tell the King that he should do in order to try to stop the fire?

WORD ATTACK SKILLS

Match each word to its correct definition to create a glossary.

Glossary

Words

✔ lighters
✔ endeavour
✔ combustible
✔ loth

Definitions

✔ unwilling or unenthusiastic
✔ to attempt, or to try
✔ capable of burning or catching fire
✔ flat-bottomed boats, used for transport on rivers or in shallow water

---

EXERCISE 2.7

Anne Frank and Samuel Pepys both describe a fire.

Samuel Pepys's diary focuses on the events and people involved. Anne Frank's is more focused on thoughts and feelings.

Write a passage comparing the impact of the different approaches. Use quotations and examples from the extracts to support your interpretations.

Key skills

Planning a diary entry

You are going to plan and write a diary entry. Diary entries are not always about historical events or life-threatening fires! They are an interesting way to explore the small details of everyday life, and to remember important, funny or surprising moments in your life.

Activity 2.5

Think of a few different events or memories from your own life that you found interesting, surprising or memorable.

Discuss each of them with a partner and decide which you would be able to turn into an interesting diary extract.

Activity 2.6

1   Working with a partner, imagine that you are taking part in a one-to-one television interview and give an account of a significant experience in your life. For example, you could choose to talk about your greatest sporting achievement.
    As you talk, your partner, who is playing the part of the interviewer, asks you questions which allow you to explore further into the importance of the episode and to express how you felt at different moments. As you speak, think about the language you use and how this helps you to get your message across. If you are being humorous, how can you show this to the interviewer with the words that you use? Once you have had your turn, swap roles and interview your partner. As the interviewer, adapt your responses and questions to the interviewee. For example, if they are being humorous, how can you show you have understood this with your questions?

2   Now work together to jot down the key experiences, details and emotions connected with your chosen event or memory.
    Discuss the appropriate **tone**:
    - humour
    - excitement
    - surprise
    - courage …
    Make some brief notes to help plan your extended writing.

KEY WORD

tone what the author feels or wants the reader to feel about something. Tone can be humorous, dark or angry, for example

HINT

Remember, use each writing task to develop your handwriting. Over time your handwriting should become easier to read and easier to write: keep track of this by comparing your current handwriting with previous writing tasks and note any areas for improvement. Keep your handwriting in a flowing style.

Graphic organisers

A diary entry may be **informal**, but **paragraphs** will help you write, and will also help a reader to follow what you have written.

Plan your paragraphs using a graphic organiser such as the one below:

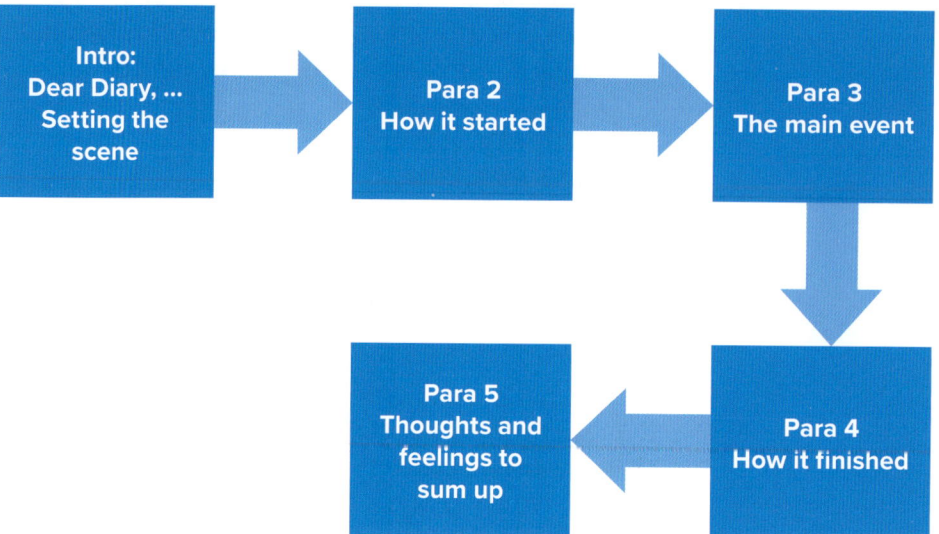

Include a first sentence for each paragraph.

Here are some sentence starters that may help:
- You won't believe what happened when …
- Suddenly, …
- Out of nowhere, …
- Just when I thought …
- I wonder what …

HINT
Look back over Anne Frank's diary. You can borrow ideas from her diary and the way she mixes description of external events with internal emotions.

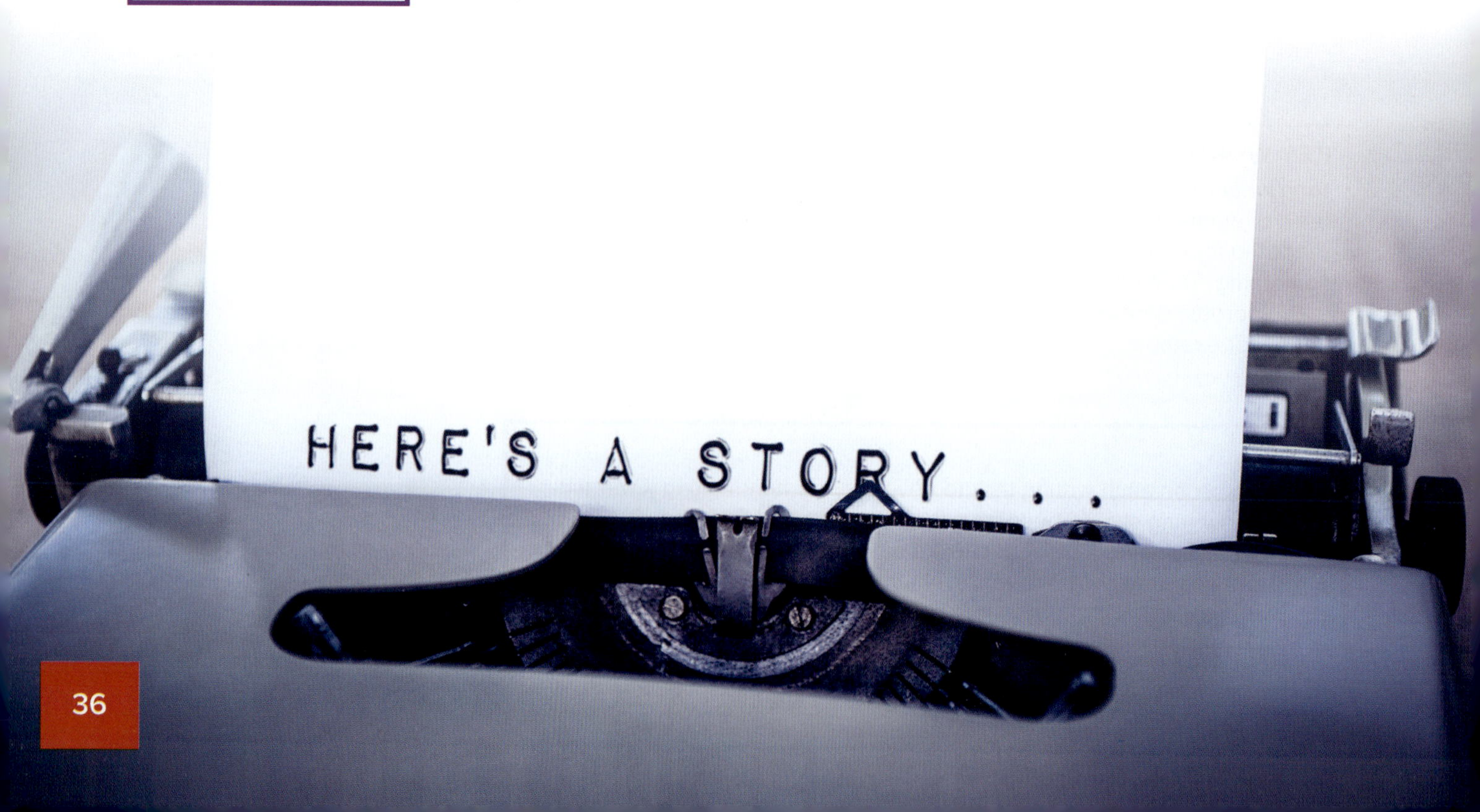

HERE'S A STORY...

Dashes

The **dash** has a variety of uses. It is often used in a diary, as it can show how one thought leads to another.

Its main use is to indicate an interruption to the main structure of a sentence, for example by an afterthought or by words interjected into the sentence. A dash is placed before and after these words – unless the interruption comes at the end of a sentence, when a full stop, question mark or exclamation mark replaces the second dash. For example:

> She showed me her new dress – very nice it was too – that her parents had given her for her thirteenth birthday.
>
> She showed me her new dress that her parents had given her for her thirteenth birthday – and very nice it was too!

Another use of the dash is to indicate a sudden dramatic end to a sentence:

> 'I'll tell you who the culprit was,' said the headteacher. 'It was – the school librarian.'

Finally, a dash can be used to show when a word or sentence is incomplete:

> The police made sure the identity of Mr K– was kept secret.
>
> 'Help. Help, I'm –' he shouted, but he fell off the ladder before I could reach him!

EXERCISE 2.8

Write some draft sentences for each paragraph of your diary extract.

Try including a dash in each sentence – to show how your thoughts may jump around a little when writing a diary.

Commas

In Checkpoint 7 we looked at different occasions when commas should be used. Now we are going to look at one further use of the comma. This use is a particularly tricky one.

A comma is used to separate from the rest of the sentence a group of words that act as an **adjective** (known as an adjectival phrase or adjectival clause) and that begin with 'who', 'whom', 'which' or 'that' *but only when this group of words has a non-defining function.*

Here are some examples to help you understand what this means and how the 'rule' works. In the following sentence, the words in italics function together as an adjective describing the car:

The car, *which was old and rusty*, belonged to the school teacher.

The words *which was old and rusty* give us additional information about the car, but we do not need this information to understand the main point of the sentence (that the car belonged to the teacher).

Now look at this sentence:

The car *that was involved in the robbery* belonged to the teacher.

This time the words in italics define the car and are essential to the meaning of the sentence – without them we would not know which car is being talked about.

EXERCISE 2.9

All of the sentences below contain phrases or clauses which act as adjectives.

Explain carefully how putting commas around these groups of words affects the meaning of each sentence.

1   Her sister who goes to my school is a good friend of mine.

2   We hope that our sponsored walk will raise a lot of money for local charities which help sick children.

3   The children who are wearing school uniform are in Year 8.

4   The students who answered all the questions correctly were let off their homework.

5   My bedroom which is painted cream badly needs decorating.

Using commas in your extended writing

EXERCISE 2.10

1   Write a further draft complex sentence for each paragraph that you have planned for your diary.

2   Use commas to insert an adjectival phrase into each sentence.

Writing

Write and evaluate

EXERCISE 2.11

Look back through your plan, including the draft sentences you have written.

You should find that you have plenty of material for a first draft.

Collect your sentences and develop each paragraph into a more detailed piece of writing. Use a range of simple, compound, complex and compound-complex sentences to make your writing varied and create effects.

Make sure you include the following features:
- Informal register
- Dashes to show thoughts leading on to other thoughts
- Events mixed in with thoughts and feelings

WORD ATTACK SKILLS

Go back and proofread your first draft. Pick up to three words and, using a thesaurus, suggest alternatives that might improve your writing.

Activity 2.7

1 Write your final piece.
2 Share your final diary entry with a partner and discuss which aspects achieve the goal you set in the planning stage.

HINT

Proofread your work and if necessary write or type a final draft without errors before you share it with others.

Reviewing

Reflect on your learning in this chapter.

Reading

- Which text did you find most engaging: Anne Frank's or Samuel Pepys's?
- Are you interested in reading any more diary-type texts?
- Some novels are written in the form of a diary. Why would an author choose to write a fictional diary?
- What strategies have you learned for understanding older texts?

Speaking and listening

- How have your language skills developed to enable you to express your thoughts and feelings?
- What speaking and listening skills did you develop?
- Did you work successfully as part of a group? Could you improve as a group in any way?

Writing

- Do you enjoy writing? Why?
- Did you find it helpful to plan your writing before beginning? Will you use a visual organiser next time you write?
- Did you use dashes in your writing?

Key skills

- How many new words have you added to your vocabulary? Can you list five or more?
- Discuss your answers and ideas with your classmates and your teacher.

Further reading

If you enjoyed reading these extracts, you might enjoy:
- *Artichoke Hearts* by Sita Brahmachari
- *I Capture the Castle* by Dodie Smith
- *Diary of a Wimpy Kid* by Jeff Kinney
- *Planet Omar: Accidental Trouble Magnet* by Zanib Mian
- Pliny the Younger's letters

Reading
★ A legend from Malaysia
★ An ancient story from India
★ Modern myths and legends

Speaking and listening
★ An extract about myths and legends in the modern world
★ A discussion about a film or game based on mythology
★ A debate about fantasy and realism
★ Performing a dramatised reading of a myth or legend

THE MAKING OF MYTHS AND LEGENDS

Writing
★ A report on a class debate about fantasy and realism
★ Your own modern myth or legend

Key skills
★ Spelling plurals
★ Suffixes
★ Working in a group

LET'S TALK
Work in a group.

■ Tell your group your favourite (or least favourite) traditional myth or legend. Briefly say what the myth or legend is about and why you like it or don't like it. If you can, say where it comes from too.

■ Can you name any modern legends? Why have they become legends do you think?

Speaking and listening

Share ideas and views about myths and legends

The following extract explains the origins of myths and legends. Though both genres are traditional stories, they can be categorised as **fantasy** fiction.

> ### Activity 3.1
>
> Skim-read the following extract and discuss what it is about.

Myths, legends and mythologising

Have you heard people say 'Oh that's just a **myth**!' and 'She's awesome – what a **legend**!'

The word 'myth' comes from the Ancient Greek language from the word *mûthos* which means a story that is told by word of mouth. Stories were told over and over again by many generations and they became well known. And that is also one way in which modern 'myths' are created. People repeat stories and **embellish** them as they do so. Sometimes they add or change events in the stories. Ordinary events are turned into more exciting stories this way. We call this **mythologising**. Today, of course, the stories are not only spread by word of mouth, they are also spread by social media and internet sites.

As you know, myths and legends are traditional stories about **heroic** (and unheroic) people and deeds in the past. They have characters and a plot, like any other story. The origins of famous myths and legends are often lost in the mists of time. However, the modern world, with the help of technology, has used these ancient myths and legends to create a popular **culture** of heroes and superheroes in different media which include film, television and games. Sometimes these 'new' stories are based on real historical figures and events. There is the legend of the Trojan War for example, with heroes like Achilles who fought in the war. A Trojan war did take place a long time ago, but the stories about it have been **romanticised**.

People who have become famous because of their scientific genius, sporting or musical achievements have become modern myths and legends as myths are created around them. Think of the scientist Albert Einstein, the composer Mozart and the tennis player Serena Williams. They have all become legends in their own time.

DID YOU KNOW?

Modern business uses many brand names from ancient myths and legends.
The sports brand Nike is named after the Greek goddess of victory.
There is a personal care brand called Dove. A dove was a symbol of Aphrodite.
Do you know any other brand names that come from mythology?

Activity 3.2

Listen to the audio about myths and legends in the modern world.
- What point of view does this speaker express?
- Do you agree or disagree?

Write down words that the speaker uses to express their point of view. You can use them later in a debate.

Spotlight on: listening

When you listen to audio there are no visual clues to help you understand. You need to concentrate on what you hear.
- Listen for key words. These are often the names of people and places.
- What is the speaker's view or opinion about the topic? Listen for words that may be used to present views, for example: *Therefore I believe that …, While it may be true that … , I think that …*
- Write short questions to answer when you listen to the text again.

LET'S TALK

Work in a group. Think about books, TV series and films that have become popular modern myths and legends.

- Who are the characters? Are any of them based on characters from ancient myths and legends that you know?
- Are the main characters men or women?
- What are the plots about?

- How were the films created? Are they acted or animated?
- Why do you think these films have been so successful?
- What does it take to create a modern myth or legend?

EXERCISE 3.1

Write a paragraph about a book, film or TV series that has mythical or legendary characters. Describe two of the main characters and say what you like and dislike about them.

Reading

Traditional myths and legends

Activity 3.3

There are many legends about Langkawi, which is an island in Malaysia.

1 Read the first paragraph of 'The legend of Mahsuri' and tell a partner briefly what this legend is about: the basic plot, characters, setting and **theme**.

2 Then read the whole extract by yourself and tell your partner more about the characters and the plot.

HINT

Use these reading strategies to get the main ideas of the text before you look for details.

- Read the first paragraph.
- Look for names of people and places.
- Make notes of key events. Verbs may give you clues to these.

Spotlight on: myths and legends

Myths and legends have features, like other works of fiction. As you read, think of the features such as *plot, character, setting, point of view, style* and *theme*.

WORD ATTACK SKILLS

Work out the meaning of the highlighted words in the context of the extract. Then check their meaning in a dictionary.

✔ conspiracy
✔ troubadour
✔ ceremonial
✔ generations

'The legend of Mahsuri'

According to legend, Mahsuri, the third daughter of Pandak Mayah, lived during the reign of Sultan Abdullah Mukarram Shah II, the ruler of Kedah between 1762 and 1800. She was one of the most beautiful women in all of Langkawi. She died in tragic circumstances after being accused of a crime of which she was totally innocent. She was the victim of a **conspiracy** planned by her own mother-in-law, Wan Mahora, who was jealous of Mahsuri's beauty and fame.

Mahsuri had married a young warrior, Wan Durus, who was the son of the chieftain of Langkawi, Datuk Seri Kerma Jaya. Soon after their wedding, Wan Durus had to leave his wife to fight in the war with Siam. During her husband's absence, Mahsuri gave birth to a baby boy, Wan Hakim. She had also befriended Deramang, a young **troubadour** who was visiting Langkawi and staying with her family. This gave Wan Mahora the opportunity she had been waiting for and she spread the rumour that Mahsuri was unfaithful to her husband.

Despite being Mahsuri's father-in-law, the chieftain of Langkawi, Datuk Seri Kerma Jaya, was so taken in by Mahora's lies that he sentenced Mahsuri to death, despite her passionate pleas of innocence.

No one believed Mahsuri's pleas and, as was the custom, she was executed with the **ceremonial** dagger. It is said that at the time of her death, white blood could be seen flowing from the wound made by the dagger. Other accounts of the execution state that a white mist arose and covered the spot where her body lay as if the earth were mourning her fate. The reports of these strange happenings have been taken by many people as evidence of her innocence.

With her dying breath, Mahsuri laid a curse on the island of Langkawi. She predicted that, as a punishment for the injustice against her, Langkawi would not prosper and would suffer seven **generations** of bad luck.

No one can say for sure whether the curse came true or whether the story of Mahsuri was a myth, a legend or a true account. We do know that in the years following her death, Langkawi was invaded and devastated by the army of Siam, Datuk Seri Kerma Jaya and his entire family were killed, and all rice fields and **granaries** were burnt and destroyed.

Even now, what appear to be burnt grains of rice are found at Padang Matsirat, a town in Langkawi. Many people, however, consider that the curse has been lifted because life on the island is happy and prosperous.

EXERCISE 3.2

Write your answers to these questions, then discuss them with your partner.

1 What were the legendary signs that Mahsuri was innocent?

2 According to the extract, what suggestions are there that there may be some truth in this legend?

3 Langkawi has now become a popular tourist destination. Do you think that the legend may in any way help the popularity of the resort? Give your reasons.

Activity 3.4

The story of Rama and Sita is an ancient story which is related to the festival of Diwali, the Festival of Light. This festival marks the triumph of light over darkness and good over evil.

Before you read the story that follows, have a class discussion and share what you know about this story.

- What is it about?
- Where does it come from?
- What is its cultural importance?

Then read this story on your own or listen to a reading of the story on the audio. Remember to listen or read for the main ideas first.

'Rama and Sita' (1)

Prince Rama, a great warrior, was married to the beautiful Sita.

Prince Rama's father, the king, wanted his son to become king after he died, but Rama's wicked stepmother tricked him into sending Rama away into the forest. Sita accompanied her husband despite Rama begging her to stay safely in the palace while he was in exile. Sita loved Rama deeply and said it was a thousand times better to be in the forest with Rama than live in the palace without him.

So Rama and Sita went to live a simple and quiet life in a humble cottage deep in the forest.

It wasn't long before their peaceful life was disturbed. One day, the demon king, Ravana, spied Sita walking in the forest. Ravana was the most terrifying of all the demons: he had ten pairs of arms, ten heads, fiery red eyes and a mouth full of sharp yellow fangs. He was so smitten by Sita's beauty that he decided to capture her and make her his wife.

It happened that, one day, Rama and Sita saw a wonderfully beautiful deer as they walked through the forest. Its skin was a beautiful golden colour and shone like the sun, its silver antlers shone brightly, its hooves were shiny black and its eyes were as blue as **sapphires**.

Sita was struck by the deer's beauty and immediately asked Rama to catch it for her so that she could look after it. Rama was worried that the deer was conjured up by a demon to cause trouble for them but finally agreed to her pleas and went off in pursuit of the deer.

Now that Sita was alone, Ravana could carry out his plan. He swooped down in his chariot pulled by the ugliest winged monsters imaginable and quickly dragged Sita into it. Although in great terror, Sita kept her wits about her and dropped pieces of her jewellery (her gold anklets, earrings and glittering scarf), hoping that Rama would find them and follow the trail she left. In the forest below, a white monkey saw the shining treasure fall from the sky and thought the stars were falling.

GLOSSARY

sapphire – a gemstone which can be different colours, blue being the most valuable

Without knowing what had happened to his wife, Rama continued to pursue the beautiful deer and finally caught it. Immediately, the deer transformed into a fearful demon and flew off into the sky. Rama feared for Sita's safety and rushed back to the cottage. Realising Sita had gone, he retraced their steps from earlier in the day and eventually discovered the trail of jewellery.

EXERCISE 3.3

What have you understood of the story so far? Recap the main points in your mind.

1   Why did Rama have to live in the forest and why did Sita accompany him there?
2   When Sita was captured by Ravana, what did she do to help Rama find her?

'Rama and Sita' (2)

As he was following the trail, Rama met with Hanuman, the white monkey. Hanuman was an important figure as he was king of the monkeys. He took Rama to a great cave in the hills where the monkeys had their city. Hanuman called all the monkeys of the city to a meeting in the great stone square in the city and also arranged for messages to be sent to all the monkeys in the world. Twenty-three million monkeys from woods and caves throughout the world flocked to the monkey city accompanied by their friends, the bears. After Hanuman told them what had happened, they set out to search the world to find Sita.

Finally, Hanuman himself found the island on which Sita was held captive. Although he had many monkeys and bears with him, they could not reach the island because of the great powerful waves of the sea that surrounded it. Hanuman, who was the son of the wind god, used his powers and, taking a great breath, leapt from the highest hill into the clouds and flew over the rough seas to land on the island and find Sita sitting alone near the palace. She was refusing to marry Ravana.

Sita was greatly pleased to see Hanuman and gave him a pearl from her hair to give to Rama as a token of her love and to show that she was unharmed. Hanuman leapt back from the island and returned with his army of monkeys and bears to tell Rama of what he had found.

The great waves of the sea still prevented Rama and his forces from reaching the island where Sita was, so they began to build a bridge out of rocks, grass and sand. The squirrels of the woods and all the animals of all shapes and sizes helped with building the bridge. This soon stretched for a hundred miles and all the animals charged across to the island.

A great and terrible battle between the host of animals and the evil demons followed. The battle lasted many days until finally Rama came face to face with Ravana. Rama used his bow and arrows to shoot the heads of Ravana but a new one grew whenever he chopped one of them off. At last he picked up a special bow and arrow that the sky god had made for him. He fired the arrow which was guided by the gods of wind and fire; it pierced Ravana's heart and a great flash of light was given off as Ravana fell dead.

→

This was the end of the rule of the demons and there were great celebrations throughout the world. Rama and Sita returned as king and queen to their own country. The people welcomed them with flags and garlands and the gods showered them with flowers. Every home in the city placed an oil lamp in their window to show their gratitude. Rama and Sita ruled the country in peace and harmony for many years.

EXERCISE 3.4

1 Who was Hanuman? Explain using your own words what he did to help find Sita.

2 After Hanuman had found Sita, why was Rama still unable to rescue her?

3 Using your own words, explain in detail how Rama was finally able to rescue Sita and to defeat Ravana.

Activity 3.5

Work in a pair and discuss these questions.

1 What is the moral of this story?

2 What is the style of the story? Is it narrative or descriptive? Would you call it a myth or a legend? Explain your answers.

3 Talk about the point of view of the writer. Who tells the story? Do you think the writer wants you to believe the story?

EXERCISE 3.5

Read this paragraph from Rama and Sita again. Look at the language used and answer the questions.

Now that Sita was alone, Ravana could carry out his plan. He swooped down in his chariot pulled by the ugliest winged monsters imaginable and quickly dragged Sita into it. Although in great terror, Sita kept her wits about her and dropped pieces of her jewellery (her gold anklets, earrings and glittering scarf), hoping that Rama would find them and follow the trail she left. In the forest below, a white monkey saw the shining treasure fall from the sky and thought the stars were falling.

1 What does the verb 'swooped' suggest or tell us about Ravana?

2 Which words are used to describe the monsters?

3 Monsters are usually ugly in myths and legends. Do you think monsters need to be ugly?

4 How does the author describe Sita's jewellery?

5 By saying that Sita 'kept her wits about her', what does the author suggest about her character?

Activity 3.6

Work in a group. Compare the story of Rama and Sita with the legend of Mahsuri.

Record your notes in a table like the one below or make a mind map with your ideas.

	Mahsuri (a legend)	Rama and Sita (a myth)
Main characters		
Setting		
Plot		
Style		
Point of view		
Theme (including possible lesson or moral)		
Language used		

LET'S TALK

Work in a group. Take turns as a group to present your comparisons to other groups.

- Explain the features of each story and say why it is considered a myth or a legend.
- Describe the comparisons you have made.
- Discuss which story you enjoyed the most and say why.

EXTENSION

Tell a traditional myth or a legend to your class or group. Make it sound as interesting as possible.

Speaking and listening

Creating modern myths and legends

Authors can create myths and legends in many ways. They can create exciting characters – good and bad, human and non-human – and describe their actions in exaggerated and descriptive language.

Some authors borrow characters and names from other languages or older stories. The author J.R.R. Tolkien made up wonderful-sounding names using words from old English. One of the characters in *The Lord of the Rings* is called 'Frodo', which possibly came from an Old English word 'frŏd' which meant 'wise'.

▲ Frodo, a character from *The Lord of the Rings*

Activity 3.7

Read this short film review and discuss these questions in pairs.
- How do the names sound to you? Do they give any indication of the type of character?
- Do you know where Thrace is? Does it matter?
- From books you have read or films you have seen, which character names do you remember? Why?

Share your ideas with the class after your pair discussion.

Film review: *Hercules*

In the ancient world, Hercules subdued all the bad characters – monsters and criminals. He was renowned for his strength, courage and his wisdom too. Ancient people honoured him with statues, buildings and ceremonies.

The film *Hercules*, with mega-star Dwayne Johnson in the title role, keeps alive the old legend and modernises it. Based on the graphic novel: *Hercules: The Thracian Wars*, the film is fast-paced and entertaining with some eye-popping action scenes. Hercules travels to Greece with his five loyal companions to sell his services for gold. The king of Thrace asks Hercules for help against a warlord who is threatening the kingdom of Thrace.

Filled with good and bad characters with names such as Amphiaraus, Megara, Autolycus, Atalanta and Rhesus, the film has been a resounding success at the box office, confirming the popularity of this modern type of legend.

Quests

Quests are adventures or journeys in search of something – it could be something physical like treasure or something metaphorical or unquantifiable, like a quest for self-discovery.

Have you read any books or watched any films about quests? Perhaps you have played quest games too. Tell your group or class about your favourite (or least favourite) quest stories or games.

Elements of traditional myths and legends have crossed over into popular culture and are seen in films and popular games. *Game of Thrones* uses elements from Old Norse myth such as ravens and wolves, as well as the idea of the long winter. The themes of films such as *Star Wars* and *Thor* rely on good male and female heroes who set out on quests to defeat evil villains and monsters. Themes such as a quest for freedom and a rise to a better way of life are also common.

In some older stories, such as the stories about Perseus and Andromeda, the male hero sets out to save a beautiful young woman who is in trouble. Popular culture today has strong female heroes such as Nakia, Okoye and Shuri in *Black Panther* and Wonder Woman, who links back to the Amazons of Greek mythology.

LET'S TALK

Work in a group and discuss a modern film or game that has some basis in mythology or legends. Through research and discussion, answer the following questions.
1. What is the theme(s)?
2. Which elements are drawn from older myths or legends?
3. Does the film or game have a lesson to teach us?
4. What role do women play in the film or game? Are the heroes all men or do women play heroic and important roles too?
5. Why do you think people enjoy the film or the game?

Key skills

Spelling plurals

Another cause of confusion for people learning to express themselves in English is how to form the plurals of **nouns**. Here is a list of the main ways in which nouns in English change from singular to plural:

- The most common way of forming the plural of a noun is by adding -*s* to the singular form: *book* – *books*; *house* – *houses*.
- Sometimes the plural is formed by adding -*es*: *dress* – *dresses*; *tomato* – *tomatoes*; *potato* – *potatoes*.
- Less common, but worth remembering, is adding -*en* to the singular form: *ox* – *oxen*; *child* – *children*.
- The -*y* at the end of the singular form may change to -*ies*: *lady* – *ladies*; *baby* – *babies*.
- The -*fe* at the end of the singular may change to -*ves*: *wife* – *wives*; *knife* – *knives*.
- Vowels in the middle of the singular form may change: *goose* – *geese*; *mouse* – *mice*.
- Some words do not change at all between singular and plural: *sheep*; *deer*; *species*; *salmon*.
- Some words that have entered English from other languages have kept their plural form in the original language: *addendum* – *addenda*; *crisis* – *crises*; *formula* – *formulae*; *phenomenon* – *phenomena*.
- Some imported foreign words have adopted English plural forms: *octopus* – *octopuses*; *syllabus* – *syllabuses*.

EXERCISE 3.6

Turn the words in italics in the following sentences into the plural form.

Note that it may be necessary to change other parts of the sentence to be grammatically correct.

1. I have to make an appointment to see the dentist as my *tooth* aches.
2. The *monkey* was a very mischievous creature.
3. The mystery *bacterium* caused an unpleasant illness.
4. The insect became disturbed and its *antenna* began to twitch.
5. This *fish* lives and feeds on the sea bed.

Speaking and writing

A debate about fantasy and realism

HINT

Think about what visual aids you could use. Will speakers need prompts? Should key ideas be summarised for the audience? What is the best way to do this?

Activity 3.8

You are going to have a debate. The subject of the debate is:

There is no real value in fantasy. It's better to engage with realistic fiction.

1   Before you start, you need to agree on how you are going to conduct the debate.
    You need to agree on:
    - who will chair the debate
    - who will introduce the debate and the speakers
    - how many people will speak *for* the topic
    - how many people will speak *against* it
    - how much time each speaker will be given
    - who the main speakers will be
    - who will keep track of time
    - how the final vote will be conducted.

2   Once you have decided on the roles, you will need some time to do research. The speakers and the other participants should all have some information to share. Be prepared to support or argue against the topic. Have ideas, examples and supporting arguments ready.

EXERCISE 3.7

Write a short, clear report on the debate you had in class. Your report should be about 250–300 words and be written in formal language. In your report:
- State what the topic was.
- Summarise two of the arguments for the topic and two of the arguments against the topic.
- In your conclusion, say who won the debate and what you think about the result.

KEY WORD

script the written text of a video, play, film or book

Activity 3.9

In your group, present a dramatised reading of a myth or legend that you have enjoyed reading.

In order to appeal to your audience, you could use some props or costumes but the focus of your presentation should be on the reading of the script. You might find it helpful for one of the group to perform as narrator.

HINT

Note that a dramatised reading is not the same thing as an acted stage performance. Dramatised readings focus on the reading of the **script** and usually nothing else, while stage performances use costumes, props, sets, gestures and a stage to perform a text.

Reading and writing

Modern legends about places

Modern myths and legends have been created to explain mysterious events.

You are going to read about two of these mysteries and consider how and why they have been created.

> **Activity 3.10**
>
> Before you read the first extract, read the title and respond to it quickly.
> - What is this about?
> - What does the title make you feel or think about?

> **WORD ATTACK SKILLS**
> Work out the meanings of the following words from the context if you can:
> - ✔ livestock
> - ✔ mutilation
> - ✔ sanction

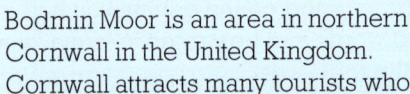

'The Beast of Bodmin Moor'

A mysterious cat-like creature with yellow eyes and long sharp teeth … It prowls around at night and attacks farm animals. It's been known to chase people too … What is it? It's the Beast of Bodmin Moor. Or maybe the Beasts of Bodmin Moor. A modern myth or is it true?

Bodmin Moor is an area in northern Cornwall in the United Kingdom. Cornwall attracts many tourists who come to enjoy the natural beauty and history. And since the late 1970s they have also been able to enjoy a local myth. How has this myth been created?

In 1978 farmers near Bodmin Moor reported the loss of some **livestock**. The livestock seemed to have suffered **mutilation** of the sort that could have been carried out by a wild creature with sharp claws and teeth. Something like a panther perhaps – dark, very fast and known to slink around at night? But there are no panthers in the UK. So theories started to emerge. Some said that it was an animal that had been kept illegally in a private zoo. Perhaps the animal had been released into the wild to escape **sanction** from the authorities? And now the animal lived on Bodmin Moor. Perhaps it was a puma rather than a panther? Eventually there was an official investigation into the matter. The investigators announced that the evidence was not verifiable.

Shortly after the investigation there were further rumours about a cat-like creature roaming around at night. And then a young boy found a skull. The skull was of a cat-like animal – a leopard! It was sent off for analysis. Speculation reached new heights! The result? Yes, it was the skull of a leopard, but the skull came from an imported rug. (Animal skin rugs with attached heads used to be popular!) And then, a few years later, a video clip emerged

EXERCISE 3.8

1 Using information from the extract, describe Bodmin Moor and the mythical Beast of Bodmin Moor.

2 According to the extract, what evidence is there that the Beast of Bodmin Moor is real?

3 What do you think is a likely explanation for the events that started the myth?

4 Write a summary of the different accounts of the Beast of Bodmin Moor in your own words.

of a young black jaguar roaming at night around the moor. At last there was real evidence of the existence of the Beast of Bodmin Moor.

Or was it? Where was the video taken? Who took it? Does it matter? A modern myth had been created. People who visit the area claim to hear or see this mysterious creature and others come many miles to look for it.

LET'S TALK

1 Talk about the style of the extract you have read.
  - Is it formal or informal?
  - Why do you think the writer used this style?
  - Does the style relate to the writer's point of view? What is that point of view?

2 Imagine that you work for the Cornish Tourism Board.
  - What would your attitude be to the myth of the Beast of Bodmin Moor?
  - Would you promote the myth? If so, why and how?

EXERCISE 3.9

One of the most famous legends of modern times concerns the strange happenings in an area of the North Atlantic Ocean called the Bermuda Triangle.

Do you know anything about the Bermuda Triangle? Think about how a modern-day legend might differ from a traditional legend, then read the following text carefully.

The Bermuda Triangle

The Bermuda Triangle is an imaginary and undefined region in the western part of the North Atlantic Ocean that is not on any official map. It is a place where a number of aircraft and ships are said to have disappeared under mysterious circumstances.

Two incidents in the area, both involving military craft, started the legend. The first event occurred in 1918 when a ship, the *USS Cyclops*, which was **en route** from Brazil to the USA, disappeared inside the Bermuda Triangle. No traces were found of the ship or the people who were on board. Then nearly 30 years later a squadron of bombers called Flight 19 also disappeared in the Bermuda Triangle. Again, no wreckage was ever found.

Unusual features about the area have been noted in the past and other ships and planes have simply vanished without trace within the imaginary triangle. However, it was only in 1964 that the area got its name. A journalist wrote an article for a magazine about the disappearance of Flight 19 in an area that he called The Bermuda Triangle and the legend making began in earnest. Ten years later the publication of a book on the subject promoted the legend. Stories were told about missing travellers and about giant sea monsters living in the area. Some even suggested that the travellers were abducted by creatures from space.

But there was no real evidence and the truth of the disappearances may have more to do with human error. Lieutenant A.L. Russell, in the US Coast Guard's official response to Bermuda Triangle inquiries, wrote: 'It has been our experience that the combined forces of nature and the unpredictability of mankind outdo science-fiction stories many times each year.'

Unusual features of the area

The Bermuda Triangle region has some unusual features.

First of all, it's one of only two places on Earth where true north and magnetic north line up. This makes compass readings difficult. The other place where this occurs is the so-called 'Devil's Sea' which is off the east coast of Japan.

It must also be remembered that the sea is very, very deep in the area. The sea floor is about 5,800 metres down and even goes as deep as 8,230 metres at one point. This great depth would make it very difficult to find any wreckage.

There are strong water currents as well as dangerous reefs in the region.

The weather in this part of the world also presents dangers. **Hurricanes** are the biggest issue. The Gulf Stream travels along part of the area. This is like a big river flowing within the ocean and it can create certain weather patterns. Storms and high waves can form suddenly in the area, as a result of the atmospheric conditions. The waves can reach heights of 6 to 8 metres. There are also **waterspouts** which are particularly dangerous to ships.

Clearly this is a dangerous part of the world for travellers, but there are many who choose to believe in the legend of the Bermuda Triangle.

GLOSSARY

en route – on a journey

hurricane – tropical storm with strong winds and a lot of rain

waterspout – a column of water

EXERCISE 3.10

1. By referring to the opening paragraphs, explain, using your own words, what the mystery of the Bermuda Triangle is.

2. Explain what is meant by 'the legend making began in earnest'.

3. Using your own words, explain what theories have been put forward to explain the disappearances in the Bermuda Triangle, and how other people have responded to these theories.

4. Explain, using your own words, the comments made by Lieutenant Russell at the end of the first section of this extract.

5. From the 'Unusual features of the area' section, write a summary of what you have learned about the unusual features of the Bermuda Triangle. You should write about 50–60 words.

LET'S TALK

In small groups of three or four discuss the similarities and differences between the traditional myths and legends and the contemporary stories of the Beast of Bodmin and the Bermuda Triangle.

KEY WORD

suffix a letter or group of letters added to the end of a word (or a word stem) in order to form a new word or to alter the grammatical function of the original word

Key skills

Vocabulary and spelling

Suffixes

As you know, a **suffix** is a letter or group of letters added to the end of a word (or a word stem) in order to form a new word or to alter the grammatical function of the original word. The main function of suffixes is to create new nouns, verbs and adjectives.

Here are some examples.

Noun suffixes	Examples	Original word
-acy	privacy, numeracy	private, numerate (adjectives)
-al	proposal	propose (verb)
-ance, -ence	maintenance, evidence	maintain (verb), evident (adjective)
-dom	freedom, kingdom	free (adjective), king (noun)
Verb suffixes	**Examples**	**Original word**
-ate	irritate	irritation (noun)
-en	cheapen	cheap (adjective)
Adjective suffixes	**Examples**	**Original word**
-able, -ible	lovable, accessible	love (verb), access (noun)
-al, -ical	regional, mythical	region (noun), myth (noun)

Activity 3.11

Work in a pair.

1 Do you remember the spelling rule about what to do when a word ends in -y? Add suffixes to these words to remind yourselves:

plenty   heavy   happy

2 What other strategies can you use to remember how to spell suffixes?

3 By referring to a dictionary or by researching online (using websites such as FindTheWord.info) make a list of other words ending with the suffixes in the table above.

As you do so, try to find common links between them, for example, most words ending in -ship are likely to be abstract nouns.

Note: Be careful, however, as words ending with the same group of letters are not necessarily all formed by the addition of a suffix. The -ist at the end of saxophonist is a suffix, but the last three letters of twist are not, for example.

HINT

Using the wrong form of a suffix is one of the most common causes of spelling errors in English, in particular through the confusion of -ance /-ence, -ense/-ence or -able/-ible.

EXERCISE 3.11

Copy the word stems that follow and add what you think is the correct ending.

When you have finished, check your spellings in a dictionary and make a list of any words that you spelled incorrectly so that you can learn these.

1 Add -ance or -ence to:

| abund- | guid- | nuis- | exist- |
| dilig- | assist- | correspond- | rever- |

2 Add -ense or -ence to:

| abs- | pret- | int- | exp- |
| imm- | disp- | recomp- | off- |

3 Add -able or -ible to:

advis-	incorrig-	indefens-	vis-
illeg-	respons-	sens-	forc-
contempt-	cred-	indispens-	inexhaust-

Writing

Write your own modern myth or legend

Myths and legends do not belong only to the distant past; events happening in the present day could well become legendary in the future. You are going to write your own modern myth or legend. Read the notes below before you begin.

How should I organise my writing?

When writing stories containing accounts of heroic events and characters, you should produce a clear narrative **structure** that your readers can follow easily. It is important to remember that the stories you are telling should focus on the main events and should have a beginning, middle and end.

Begin by describing how the episode came about. Or, if you are describing a legendary character, you could start with details of where they were born, went to school and so on. You could then go on to describe the event itself, or the significant details of the central character's life. Conclude with describing the aftermath of the mythical episode, or what the heroic character did after the event.

Although the account reaches its climax with the main event, it is important you include sufficient information about what follows so that the readers don't lose interest before the end of your story.

Remember that to mythologise an event you need to:

- embellish or exaggerate certain parts of an event or certain features of a character
- think carefully about your choice of words.

> **KEY WORDS**
> **structure** the way a text is organised so that it usually has a beginning, middle and end
> **purpose** the reason or intention for writing the piece, e.g. to amuse, to inform, to entertain

Activity 3.12

1 Think of an actual event that has happened in your local community that could be developed into a legend. Your **purpose** is to inform others about achievements in your community. Your legend should be 400–500 words long.
2 Write about an event of which you have some direct knowledge and that you imagine might achieve legendary status in your community over the years. Think of someone who possesses interesting or remarkable qualities – it could be a school friend who has performed a great sporting achievement (winning the 100m event in the school's sports or, as a more humorous topic, eating a large number of sausages in a record time). Discuss this as a class or in a group. Brainstorm appropriate ideas.
3 Work alone and draft an account of the event as if it were a legend.
4 Then share your stories in a group. Read them aloud and talk about them. Decide which one or two legends would work best.
5 As a group, refine the selected story or stories. Read the edited legend aloud to the rest of the class.

HINTS

■ Focus on what might appear to be an everyday event and then, by the way you describe it, make it into a heroic episode.

■ Do not rehash or imitate the adventures of super-hero characters in blockbuster films as this is not what is required.

■ It is best not to overcomplicate your content by including too many episodes. If you choose to describe an action or achievement that is legendary, it is best to concentrate on giving a clear and detailed account of just this action and the part your hero plays in it, and then make clear why it is worthy of legendary status.

■ If you decide to concentrate on the legendary status of one person, rather than an important episode in that person's life, then it would be best to select and summarise their major achievements, and why they are worthy of note, without going into great detail about any one of them.

EXTENSION

1 Work in a small group and compile a small collection of real local myths. Some members of the group could explore ancient myths and others look at contemporary ones. If you have the resources available, you might also want to investigate whether the stories you have found relating to your country have similarities to those found in other parts of the world.

2 Now rewrite the stories and make a collection of them. You could do this as a presentation on a tablet or computer or you could print out the stories and put them in a folder.

■ Although the story may be many hundreds of years old, you should tell it in such a way that it appeals to your contemporaries.

■ Your story will be one of four or five written by different authors, all of which should be of similar length. You might decide in your group that it would be useful for each of you to write an introduction to your story in which you summarise the research you have done and give some further background information to help the readers understand important details. These introductions should be about one page long.

KEY WORD

epic a long narrative poem which usually tells of the heroic deeds of a person of great courage and bravery

■ You may want to take a more ambitious approach by describing the events of the story in a different order, such as starting with either the main event (the middle of your story) and then going back to the beginning and following this with the end. This is a feature of **epic** poetry, a form of poetry written in the past which deals with hugely significant legendary events in human history. Examples include Homer's account of the story of the siege of Troy. You are not being asked to produce an epic poem but starting at a point in a story other than the chronological beginning is a tried and trusted technique.

Reviewing

Reflect on your learning in this chapter.

Reading

- Which of the texts did you prefer?
- Did you enjoy the genre of myths and legends?
- Would you choose to read more from this genre?
- Write a list of the skills and techniques you learned from reading and learning about myths and legends.

Speaking and listening

- How did it feel to share your own writing or ideas with a group or a partner?
- Did it help to work with others when planning your own writing or responses?
- Did you work successfully as a group? Did you feel confident to contribute? What do you think you could improve?

Writing

- What techniques did you use in your own writing?
- What did you change between your first and second drafts? How did you decide what to change?
- What stage of the writing process do you enjoy? What do you need to work on more?

Key skills

- How many new words have you added to your vocabulary? Can you list five or more?
- Can you remember any of the spelling strategies taught in this chapter? Do they help?

Further reading

If you enjoyed reading these extracts, you might enjoy:
- *The Penguin Book of Norse Myths: Gods of the Vikings* by Kevin Crossley-Holland
- *Fairy Tales for Fearless Girls* by Anita Ganeri
- *Fairy Tales from the Brothers Grimm* by Philip Pullman
- *Treasury of Egyptian Mythology: Classic Stories of Gods, Goddesses, Monsters & Mortals* by Donna Jo Napoli

THIS IS VITAL

Reading
★ Leaflets from different charities
★ Two reports on the same subject
★ Reading for meaning and understanding

Speaking and listening
★ Working in a group to produce a leaflet
★ A class discussion about the facilities in your school
★ Pronunciation of rhyming words

Writing
★ A comparison of two leaflets
★ An information leaflet
★ A report on improving the facilities in your school

Key skills
★ Verb phrases
★ Spelling variations and pronunciation
★ Interpreting and evaluating texts

LET'S TALK

As a class, discuss where and how you prefer to obtain vital information: books, leaflets, reports, the internet? Give reasons for your preferences. Discuss which sources you consider the most reliable, and why others may not be as trustworthy.

Reading and writing

Extract: Dealing with teen anger

Dealing with teenage anger

We all feel emotions and anger is one of them. Just like pain, anger itself can indicate that what is happening around you is not acceptable or it could also be an indication that something needs to change. Teenagers are trying to make sense of lots of changes. Whether that be physical changes, changes in their emotions, or a desire to be in control, all of which can make them feel upset and angry.

How do you deal with anger in your teen?

Sometimes teens can push you too far resulting in arguments and conflicts, almost like childhood tantrums. They get flooded with emotions and are not able to think straight or listen to reason. What they need to is get their feelings out and calm down. Here are some practical tips to help you effectively deal with anger in your teen.

Stay calm

Your teen's anger may be directed by you but it may have stemmed from something which isn't related to you, for example, something that happened to them at school or outside the home.
See if there is anything they want differently from you, but try and not let their anger affect you and make you angry.

Listen to your teen

Make it your starting point to listen to them rather than trying to win the argument with them. Through listening to them you can work out what is going on beneath their anger and what they help they may need from you. You can also try and help them name the emotion or feeling they are experiencing, for example 'you sound really frustrated here' or, 'you sound really scared'.

Set limits on your teen's behaviour

Listening to your teen and helping them is not accepting their behaviour. When things have calmed down you can sit down with them and set limits on what is acceptable behaviour. You could say 'I'd like you to find a way to help you deal with your anger without shouting at me'. What do you think would help you?'

Wait until the storm is over

When calm is restored, acknowledge the strong and painful feelings your teen has had. Help them to understand what they can do to express their feelings in the future without hurting themselves or others. Sometimes, helping them recognise and accept their feelings is enough. Other times you may need to help them figure out what they need to do.

How we can help

Family Lives is always here to support you through difficult times. For support call our **confidential helpline** on 0808 800 2222, email us at **askus@familylives.org.uk** or **chat to us online**

© Family Lives
Registered company number: 3817762
Registered charity number: 1077722
Registered in England and Wales..
15-17 The Broadway, Hatfield, Hertfordshire, AL9 5HZ

Analysing language choice

Activity 4.1

Read the extract on the previous page.
Work in a group to discuss these questions.
Summarise:
- What is the main message and subject of this text?

Recognise and interpret text types:
- Who is the intended *audience* of this text?
- What is the main *purpose* of this text?
- What is the *form* of this text?

Evaluate writer's choices:
- Which organisation or layout *features* of this text stand out?
- What *language choices* has the writer made?
- How effectively do the language choices match the purpose and intended audience?

EXERCISE 4.1

Find these phrases in the text:
- 'get their feelings out'
- 'can push you too far'
- 'when things have calmed down'

These phrases are written in an informal register.

Look at the following three statements.

> It is written informally throughout.

> It is mainly informal with some formal language.

> It is mainly formal with some informal language.

Write a paragraph to justify which of these statements you agree with using evidence from the text to support your ideas.

Do you remember?

Formal language is the form of standard English that is used for business, legal and professional purposes. Formal language does not use colloquialisms or contractions, and avoids first-person pronouns such as 'I' and 'we'.

Key skills

Verb phrases

Look at this discussion between two parents:

> I try to tell her, enough is enough.

> I want to listen, I want to support her – but she makes it so hard.

There are two verbs in the first speech bubble: 'try' and 'tell'.

The verb 'to tell' is used in its infinitive form (the basic form, using 'to'). This is a verb phrase that tells you what the person is trying to do.

EXERCISE 4.2

Finish each of these verb phrases:

1 I try to jump over the ...

2 I try to remember what ...

3 I try to remind him that ...

4 I try to stay safe when ...

5 I try to hide whenever ...

Activity 4.2

With a partner, look at the different versions of the sentence below. Discuss which you think are correct and which are incorrect. Write the corrections that are needed.

1 I try to tell them enough's enough.

2 She tries to tell them enough's enough.

3 We try to tell them enough's enough.

4 He try to tell them enough's enough.

5 You tries to tell them enough's enough.

6 They try to tell them enough's enough.

EXERCISE 4.3

There is another form like this in the text:

> they seem to ignore ...

Complete each of these sentences with an infinitive verb phrase

1 They seem to ...

2 She hopes to ...

3 You always forget to ...

4 I really want to ...

5 He needs to ...

EXERCISE 4.4

Complete each negative form of these sentences.

1 a I do not try to ...

  b I try not to ...

2 a I do not need to ...

  b I need not ...

Writing and speaking

Choosing verbs for purpose

EXERCISE 4.5

Look at these examples. They are all incorrect. The tense of the infinitive verb phrase cannot change.

> I try to telling her that
>
> I try to told her that
>
> I try to be telling her that
>
> I try to should tell her that
>
> I try to will tell her that

The main verb of the sentence may change tense.

> I wanted to …
>
> I will forget to …
>
> You should have remembered to …
>
> I was hoping to …

Write five more sentences that use an infinitive phrase. Use a different tense for each sentence and use some negative phrases.

EXTENSION

Experiment with adding adverbs to make your sentences more interesting.

Infinitive verb forms can form part of an adjective phrase, for example:

> It's easy **to think that** …
>
> It's difficult **to see that** …

This sentence form allows the writer to adopt a viewpoint, and to show empathy with the intended audience (an understanding of their feelings).

This is a very useful technique to use in discussion, persuasion and when presenting a balanced argument. These phrases are also useful for bringing calm to a discussion when emotions are running high.

Activity 4.3

1   Discuss this statement as a group.

> Children and teenagers spend too much time on their phones or playing video games. This is a terrible thing for their development and education. It makes them rude and violent. This is why teenagers are lazy and unhelpful.

This is full of strong and emotional language. The people within your group may disagree or agree with different points.

➡

2 Now try rewriting the statement using phrases such as:

It is easy to think that …

Some people find it difficult to see why …

Many adults may agree it is simple to explain …

3 Take it in turns to read aloud your new statements. Discuss how this changes the tone and emotive nature of the arguments.

Listening and key skills

Spelling variations and pronunciation

Sometimes, helping them recognise and accept their feelings is enough.

Through listening to them you can work out what is going on beneath their anger …

'Enough' and 'through' both use the -ough spelling pattern but are pronounced differently.

WORD ATTACK SKILLS

Read aloud this list of -ough spellings:

✔ enough
✔ tough
✔ bought
✔ though
✔ through
✔ borough
✔ thought
✔ dough
✔ bough
✔ trough
✔ plough
✔ rough
✔ thorough
✔ brought
✔ cough

Work in a pair to discuss the meaning and correct pronunciation of each word.

EXERCISE 4.6

Sort the words from the Word Attack Skills box based on their pronunciation. Use a table like the one below.

Rhymes with …						
stuff	too	how	sort	off	low	drummer

EXTENSION

Write a sentence containing as many -ough words as you can. Make sure the words are used with their correct meaning. Challenge a partner to read the sentence as a tongue twister.

Activity 4.4

The word 'express' is used in the leaflet on page 62.

The 'ss' makes the sound /sh/ in the word 'expression', but a /ss/ sound in the word 'express'.

Look at these pairs of words, and come up with a pronunciation rule. When does 'ss' make the /sh/ sound and when does it make the /ss/ sound?

▪ impression   impress
▪ repression   repress
▪ discussion   discuss
▪ depression   depress

Writing

Spelling continued

Activity 4.5

1 Work with your partner to sort these words into two lists. Use a table like the one below.

- pressure
- fissure
- professor
- fussy
- fission
- mission
- massive
- lesser
- tissue
- omission
- excessive
- emission
- messily
- passed

'ss' pronounced /ss/	'ss' pronounced /sh/

2 Collect other words that use 'ss' and add them to your lists.

Confusing similar words

Many writers of English blur the meaning of what they want to say by confusing words that either sound similar or have a similar, but not exactly the same, meaning. Here are some of these words:

- avoid/prevent
- stay/live
- bring/take
- uninterested/disinterested
- bored/boring
- there/their/they're
- your/you're
- horde/hoard
- principal/principle
- affect/effect.

EXERCISE 4.7

Write sentences containing each of the words listed above to make their meaning clear. If you are in doubt about the meaning of any of the words, check in a dictionary before writing your sentences.

EXERCISE 4.8

Use a selection of these similar words to write a paragraph describing how you and your peers feel towards something, for example, how you feel about going to school or playing in a sports team.

Reading and writing

Extract: 'This little chick ...'

There are approximately 30 million egg-laying hens in the UK. Around 75% are kept in battery cages. The others are kept in 'alternative' systems such as 'barn' or 'free range'. But look at these photos. Is there really much difference?

A recently-rescued free range hen

Photo: PAWN

BATTERY HELL

In battery units, four or five hens are crammed into a space not much bigger than a microwave oven. They are barely able to move, let alone stretch their wings. Battery cages are so inhumane that they will be banned in the EU from 2012 – but that means years of suffering ahead. And the replacement, so-called 'enriched' cages, will make little difference – because a cage is still a cage and the extra space the hens will have is equivalent to the size of a postcard.

BARN MISERY

The term 'barn eggs' is used deliberately to dupe the public into thinking that the hens are kept in bright, airy conditions with fresh straw on the floor. Not true! Though uncaged, the hens are still confined to dirty, overcrowded sheds. They will never see daylight, breathe fresh air or be able to exercise their natural instincts.

Photo: Viva!

FREE RANGE?

Photo: PAWN

Many people associate 'free range' with 'cruelty-free' and assume the hens live a natural life. The reality is very different: thousands of 'free range' hens may be packed into huge sheds with limited access to the outdoors. Often, less than half of the birds roam freely into and out of the sheds because the others are simply unable to fight their way through to the exits.

MALE CHICKS KILLED

Each year in the UK, approximately 30 million day-old male chicks are gassed or tossed alive into giant industrial shredders, 'disposed of' because they are unable to lay eggs and are considered too scrawny a type of chicken for meat production.

NOT ALL THEY'RE CRACKED UP TO BE

Eggs contain saturated fat, one of the main causes of heart disease – and they are among the highest sources of dietary cholesterol. Research also indicates that eggs can inhibit the absorption of iron (needed for healthy blood, cells and nerves) and contribute to loss of calcium (necessary for healthy bones). There are no nutrients in eggs that cannot be obtained from other foods. Cutting out animal products entirely is the *really* healthy option.

Send for a free recipe pack. See reverse.

Tel 01732 364546

ANIMAL AID

www.animalaid.org.uk

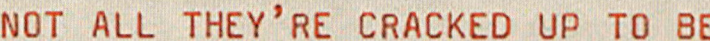

Reading for meaning and understanding

WORD ATTACK SKILLS

Find the following words in the text on page 68. From the context, or by using a dictionary or other tool, write a definition of each word:

✔ roam
✔ scrawny
✔ enriched
✔ overcrowded
✔ approximately

Write sentences containing each of these words, which demonstrate the correct meaning.

EXERCISE 4.9

The word 'battery' has a common meaning.

This is not the meaning of the word 'battery' used in the leaflet in the 'Battery hell' section.

Research and define the different meanings of the word 'battery', and highlight the correct meaning for the context of this leaflet text.

EXERCISE 4.10

Write a short summary, explaining the main subject and purpose of the text. Keep your summary factual and clear.

The subject of the leaflet 'This little chick ...' is

EXERCISE 4.11

Write your own personal response to what you have read.
- Did you understand the purpose of the text?
- How did the content make you feel?
- Do you have any strong emotions about the topic?
- Has this text changed your mind in any way?
- Do you agree or disagree with any points in the text?
- Do you believe the facts presented in the text?

Key skills

Interpreting and evaluating a text

Now it is time to interpret the approach the writer has used, and to think critically about the language techniques.

Activity 4.6

With a partner, find and copy phrases or sentences from the text on page 68 that clearly show the writer's viewpoint. Explain how the words you have chosen demonstrate the writer's opinions.

Activity 4.7

A written text may have a single purpose, or multiple purposes:
- persuade
- argue
- advise
- inform
- explain
- describe
- analyse
- review
- discuss
- narrate
- entertain

Together, choose one or more of the options from this collection to describe the purposes of the text on page 68. Use evidence from the text to justify your choices.

Activity 4.8

The text ends with the sentence:

> Cutting out animal products altogether is the really healthy option.

There are many sentences that are presented as facts in this text. Some are purely factual, but others may be examples of bias or opinion disguised as fact.

With your partner, collect a selection of sentences from the text that are presented as facts, and sort them based on these headings:
- Definitely facts
- Definitely bias
- Need more evidence to decide

Reading

Comparing multiple texts

EXERCISE 4.12

Write a detailed comparison of the two leaflets 'Dealing with teen anger' (page 62) and 'This little chick ...' (page 68) in which you look at the similarities and differences between them. Make sure that you support your comments by referring to and quoting from the content of the leaflets. For each leaflet, you should consider the following points in particular:
- the purpose of the leaflet
- its audience – who it is aimed at
- the information it contains
- its layout – for example, the use of illustrations, colour, subheadings, different fonts
- the ways in which it emphasises key points
- if there is any bias from the writer and what the impact is
- the tone of the language – in particular, the use of emotive vocabulary and the ways in which facts and opinions are conveyed to readers
- how successful the leaflet is in achieving its purpose, giving your reasons.

Writing

Writing for a specific purpose

The activities that follow will give you the opportunity to write an information leaflet and also to practise writing a report that is detailed and clearly structured, using the knowledge you have gained from the examples earlier in the chapter and the questions you have answered on them.

Writing a leaflet

Activity 4.9

Write a leaflet on one of the following topics:

- **Option A**
  A leaflet aimed at new students coming to your school. Rather than producing an 'official' type of leaflet (similar to one giving information for parents), you could produce an 'alternative' guide to the school and how to cope with the first few weeks, written from a student's perspective and aimed at other students.

- **Option B**
  A leaflet aimed at raising people's awareness of an important issue (for example, the need to look after your local environment or the importance of eating healthily). Think carefully about the audience for this leaflet – will it be for your peers (people your age) or for people of an older or younger generation?

- **Option C**
  A leaflet intended for visitors to your local area, making them aware of places, facilities and amenities that may be of interest to them during their visit.

This is an opportunity to make use of the digital facilities available to you and to work in small groups to produce a professional-looking leaflet.

Your leaflet should be written to provide information but you also want to make the readers of the leaflet feel that you understand how they feel (A), persuade your readers to support your point of view (B) or to be sufficiently interested by your description of the area that they will want to visit (C). You should therefore use **emotive language** to influence your readers' response to the content.

You should also think carefully about the structure and visual organisation of your text. Decide on the best use of the features of a leaflet for your purpose:
- headings
- diagrams
- information boxes
- captions
- slogans
- layout design.

HINT
Although leaflets appear short and simple, the language choices need to be very specific to match the purpose and intended audience.

KEY WORD
emotive language
the use of words and phrases to provoke an emotional response to a subject in the readers

Reading

Comparing two reports

Reports are spoken or written accounts of something that you have observed, heard, done or investigated. They should be **formal** in tone and focused objectively on the facts of the subject about which you are writing or speaking (not influenced by personal feelings or opinions). Reports may also include recommendations as to how particular issues can be resolved.

Here are two reports that deal with the same subject. Read both reports carefully.

Report 1: New Year Fun

Dear Headteacher

We're in class 8G and we all thought that it would be a great idea if we could organise a charity fund-raising activity. So we had a discussion and Lee (or at least, I think it was Lee but it could have been Soraya) came up with the idea that we ought to organise a New Year celebration party for the kids in the local Under 5s Playgroup. So we made arrangements with the people who run it and decided on what we would charge for admission then we all thought about what we could each do.

Anyway, all of our class arrived at the playgroup on New Year's Day and started to get things ready. We had some food and drink that we'd organised and we had some play equipment and other things that we thought we'd do, like some of the class had brought along hi-fi equipment so that there could be dancing and just after we'd got things ready it was time to start so we opened the doors and loads of little kids along with their parents came rushing in.

We didn't charge anything for admission but they had to pay to buy food and to take part in the activities. The trouble was they all wanted to do everything at once and none of them had the right money so it was hard to give them change and then the bouncy castle collapsed because too many of them were climbing on it at once and we hadn't got enough food ready and so some of the young kids started crying because they thought they wouldn't get any but eventually we got some more sandwiches and cakes and hot dogs ready and then they were happy again but it really was very chaotic at times but in the end they all went home happy and although we had a lot of clearing up to do, we were happy as well because we'd made a lot of money for charity.

Report 2: Report on charity activity

To: Headteacher, Green Trees Secondary School
From: Class 8G, Green Trees Secondary School

Background
In order to raise money for the Children in Need charity, members of Class 8G at Green Trees Secondary School arranged a New Year's Day party for the Tiny Tots Playgroup for Under 5s. The event was held at the Tiny Tots Centre in President Road from 14.00 to 16.00 hrs on 1 January.

All 26 members of Class 8G were involved and between them had organised refreshments and a range of activities suitable for the under-5 age group.

Details of the event
A large number of children from the playgroup, accompanied by their parents, attended the event. Those members of Class 8G who were supervising admission counted between 60 and 67 children attending. (Owing to the large number present at the start of the event and the fact that no admission charge was made, it was not possible for an exact count to be made.)

All of the activities and stalls provided at the event proved to be very popular with the children from the playgroup and at the end of the afternoon all the food and drink provided for them had been consumed.

The large number of children present at one time caused some problems — at one stage food ran out and there was a delay before a second round was produced. Also, there was a malfunction with the bouncy castle as a result of overcrowding and there were also some problems with providing change at some of the stalls. However, all these problems were eventually dealt with without affecting the enjoyment of those attending.

After the event had finished, Class 8G stayed behind to clear up the hall in which the event was held. In total, a profit of £377 was made which will be donated to Children in Need.

Recommendations
Although the event was successful, some points arose which should be kept in mind for any future, similar activities. The key recommendations are:
- It is important that an exact count is made of how many people are present and so it is suggested that in future tickets should be issued

in advance and handed in when visitors arrive. Accurate advance information as to the number of people likely to be present will also help in planning the amount of food needed and prevent a shortage occurring as happened this year.

- More careful supervision should be kept on activities such as the bouncy castle. In future, strict control should be kept over the number of children allowed on the activity at any one time.
- All those running stalls and other activities should be provided with a 'float' of small change before the event opens to ensure that there are no problems in dealing with visitors who do not have the exact amount of money required.

:::: **EXERCISE 4.13**

If you were the headteacher who received these reports, which would you find the more informative and why? Decide which report is less effective and then write a brief commentary on it (about 200–250 words) in which you point out particular examples of why it is not effective and give your reasons for saying so.

Key skills

Tone and register

The tone and **register** of your writing gives it its individual quality or style. For example, your tone could be formal or informal, humorous or serious. It is important that your tone stays consistent throughout each piece of writing.

One of the key features of a writer's tone and register is the **standpoint** that the writer adopts. This is the position that you, as a writer, take up in order to convey your ideas and character to the reader. The first thing to decide is whether you are going to use the first or third person to express yourself.

If you choose to write in the first person ('I was …') you are likely to establish an informal tone as you will be addressing the reader directly. This informality of tone is also likely to become apparent through the use of colloquial abbreviations (for example, 'I don't agree with what you're saying' rather than 'I do not agree with what you are saying').

If you choose to write in the third person ('It is thought that …' or 'People think …') then your tone will become more objective and impartial as you will have removed the personal element. You are therefore likely to produce a more formal piece of writing.

> **KEY WORDS**
>
> **register** how friendly (informal) or formal the language is
>
> **standpoint** the position from which a writer views and judges things

EXERCISE 4.14

Write an analysis of the language techniques used in Report 2.

Include evidence about the following points:
- vocabulary and standard English
- passive or active voice
- formal or informal tone
- use of sentence types:
  - simple
  - complex
  - compound
- intended audience
- paragraph openers and text organisation.

Writing and speaking

Planning a written task

Now it is time to write your own report. This will be addressed to your headteacher and will be on the topic of improving the facilities in your school.

Work through the following activities to plan and create your written proposal.

LET'S TALK

Address the following questions as a class discussion. Make notes during the discussion, as you can use ideas from others to inform your own writing task.

- What different facilities exist in your school?
- How do the current facilities benefit your school?
- Which facilities would benefit from improvement?
- What are the needs and interests of your students?
- Are the interests of many different students met?
- Could there be more diversity?
- What challenges may prevent the creation of new facilities.

HINT

Remember the success criteria for group discussion. Listen politely to one another and take it in turns to speak.

EXERCISE 4.15

Review your own notes from the discussion. Consider these questions individually:

- What points did you find most interesting?
- What facilities do you think would benefit the school the most?
- What did you find persuasive about the ideas you preferred?

Activity 4.10

Write three different proposals for different ideas for your writing task. Make each proposal one or two sentences only.

Review the proposals with a partner. Choose the one you feel you could write about most confidently and persuasively.

Writing, editing and evaluating

Do you remember?

Remember that the **tone** of your writing conveys your attitude towards the subject and towards your audience, and that the **register** created by the language you use should be appropriate to the formality or otherwise of your relationship with your audience.

Write a first draft

Now write a first draft of your proposal letter.

Use this organiser to plan your paragraphs:

Introduction
Give a clear and concise description of your main idea

Justify the need
Persuade your reader as to why your proposal is needed

Describe how your proposal can be achieved

Explain how the challenges can be overcome

Conclusion
Finish with a clear summary and a strong call for action or support

Write a final draft

Share your first draft with a partner.

Discuss whether the language choices are suitable in terms of:

- tone – formal or informal
- viewpoint
- standard English
- accuracy of vocabulary and punctuation.

Take advice from your partner, make some edits to your first draft, then write a final draft for your intended audience.

HINT
Word processing your work can help to streamline the revision process.

Reviewing

Reflect on your learning in this chapter.

Reading

- How do you prefer to obtain vital information? Has your opinion changed now that you've worked through Chapter 4?
- Which issues are important to you? Will you go on to research and read further information about the issues that are important to you?

Speaking and listening

- How did it feel to share your ideas with a group or a partner? Do you think your confidence to speak aloud has changed in any way since beginning Checkpoint 8?
- Did it help to work with others when planning your own writing or responses?
- Do you think you worked well as part of a small group or with a partner? What do you think you could improve?

Writing

- What techniques did you use in your own writing?
- What did you change between your first and second drafts? How did you decide what to change?
- What stage of the writing process do you enjoy? What do you need to work on more?

Key skills

- List up to five new words you have learned.
- What other key skills did you enjoy learning in Chapter 4?

Further reading

If you enjoyed reading these materials, you might enjoy:
- *Go Big: The Secondary School Survival Guide* by Matthew Burton
- *Stand Against: Prejudice* by Izzi Howell
- *This Book Will (Help) Cool the Climate* by Isabel Thomas

You can use these topics to write your own leaflets. Also look out for informative leaflets and reports around you – on noticeboards, at community centres, in shops and at school.

5 What's the source?

Reading
★ News articles
★ A sports report
★ Newspaper reports on global warming
★ Extracts from political speeches

Speaking and listening
★ Class discussion: human interest
★ Class discussion: identifying purpose
★ Listening to the news
★ Reading news articles aloud

WHAT'S THE SOURCE?

Writing
★ An article about a local sports event
★ A short news report

Key skills
★ Bias
★ Language choice
★ Literary devices
★ Political language

LET'S TALK

Discuss these questions as a class:

- What type of news do you read, listen to or watch (for example, sport, world events, health)?
- How often do you read, listen to or watch the news?
- Where do you get your news?
- What is fake news? How do you identify it?

Reading and speaking

News reports

HINT

Different readers prefer different types of news. Some people prefer short summaries of the main ideas, while others prefer detailed explanations. Some people like to read several different sources to form a better idea of events. Others prefer to rely on one source of news.

What kind of news do you prefer? Does it vary depending on the news item?

Activity 5.1

Work in a group.

1 To prepare for the activity, you will each find a short item of news (about 100–150 words) and bring it to share with the group. You can bring a written text to share or you can take notes about news that you have listened to or watched.

2 Take turns to read your news aloud to the group. Then explain briefly where you found the news (your source) and why you find it interesting.

3 As a group, discuss these questions about the news that you shared:
   - Which piece of news was the most interesting? Why?
   - Which source of news did the group use the most? Why?
   - Which sources do you think provide the most accurate news reports? How do you know this?
   - Which sources provide the most interesting news reports? What is interesting about them?

4 As a group, write up short notes to summarise your discussion and then present these to the rest of the class.

EXERCISE 5.1

Write a paragraph in which you describe the following:
- what type of news you read
- how often you read news
- which news sources you use.

Key skills

Spotlight on features of news items: headlines

The purpose of a headline is to grab the attention of the viewer or listener. To do this, headlines need to be short and punchy.

KEY WORD

headlines words printed in large letters as the title of a story in a newspaper

The language of headlines

Most **headlines** use short words whenever possible – among the most common are *deal*, *cost*, *ban*, *hit*, *clash* – and frequently use a combination of two nouns or nouns and adjectives; for example:

Petrol cost soars

Cash cut-back threat

Another feature of headline language is the use of the simple present tense of verbs and the use of the infinitive form of the verb to express the future; for example:

Inflation hits highest peak

President to call election in summer

Spotlight on features of news items: layout and visuals

News reports use photographs (with **captions**) to attract the readers' attention and to illustrate the stories and ideas in the paper. The text is set out in **columns** to make it easier to read. And some text is in bold print or in bright colours such as red and blue to catch the readers' attention. The first page of the newspaper carries the most recent and exciting news.

Activity 5.2

Work in a pair.

1 What do you expect when you see the banner on the right on your TV screen?
2 Read the following headlines. Say what you think the news is about and which ones attract you as readers.

INFLATION HITS HIGHEST PEAK

Temperatures soar!

Key roles swapped by United forwards

Clashes on street

'Ban cars' say Greens

Relief comes to stricken town

Shock announcement – 'No more live gigs!'

Is Zoom fatigue for real?

Party bombshell before election

IMPROVE YOUR MEMORY ... IN JUST 5 MINUTES

3 Now discuss the features of the headlines:
- Are any of the headlines in full sentences? If not, which parts have been left out?
- Which verb tense is used in most of the headlines?
- Why are words like 'shock' and 'bombshell' often used in headlines?
- What punctuation is used? Does it add tension or drama (shock value) to the headlines? Does it change the meaning of the headlines at all?

KEY WORDS

caption a title or explanation for a picture or illustration
columns the vertical blocks of print into which a page of a newspaper or magazine is divided

EXERCISE 5.2

1 Find two examples of headlines that you think are interesting and effective. You can use printed or online news sources.
2 Write a paragraph in which you explain briefly what the features of the headlines are.
3 Share the headline that you think is best with a group and explain why you think it works.

Activity 5.3

Work in a group.

1 Each person in the group should find a news item that is presented in a way that attracts attention. Focus on the layout and visual elements of the news. If you use a printed newspaper as a source, choose a front page.
2 Present it to your group and explain why it attracts people.
3 Compare your news item with the news item on the right which comes from a newspaper dated 1744. Look in particular at the:
- layout and the visuals
- length of the news items.

Speaking and listening

The purpose of news

Spotlight on features of news items: purpose

News items can have different purposes. A lot of the news is meant to *inform* us about events that have happened or to *narrate* events that are happening. Sometimes a news report will also *analyse* events. Journalists also give reviews of books, shows and films. Some news is simply meant to *entertain* us or to give us *advice*.

Activity 5.4

Work in a group. Go back to the news items you presented to your group. Discuss what the purpose of each news item is.

EXERCISE 5.3

Listen to the four short extracts and write down what you think the purpose of each news item is.

1 Are you caught by Clickbait?
2 Book review
3 Why we need to take action on climate change now!

KEY WORD

human interest the aspect of a story in a newspaper that describes the experiences or emotions of individuals to which readers can relate

Spotlight on features of news items: human interest

One of the most important features of newspaper reports is the **human interest** angle. In order to bring their stories to life and to appeal to the interests of their readers, journalists often include personal details about the people in their stories, even if they have no direct relevance to the events being reported.

LET'S TALK

1 Read the following short news extract and discuss how the writer has used human interest to attract readers.

> The accident was witnessed by a 17-year-old blonde youth wearing blue jeans and a red sweatshirt. The victim, Andrea Lee, 55, was taken to hospital but later discharged and returned to her $500,000 in the country.

2 Work in a group. Take one of these items of sports news and discuss how you can add human interest angles to make it more appealing to people who follow sports. Present your revised sports report to the class.
  ■ A young athlete recently won an important race or match.
  ■ The supporters of an overseas team came to watch a match in your town.
  ■ A sports competition has been cancelled due to bad weather.
  ■ Youngest ever player selected for national team.

HINT

You can make up information for this activity.

Key skills

The language of news articles

Journalists use various techniques to make their articles more interesting, for example:

- varying the **sentence openers**
- connecting sentences in different ways
- exaggeration
- a mixture of direct and reported speech.

Look for these features in the following example:

> Making her first appearance for the team, the young 17-year-old from Kenya scored the first goal and so carved her name into the history books. 'I saw my opportunity and nothing could stop me,' she said afterwards. She also said that she felt so proud. This amazing goal set off wild celebrations across the country, raising the hopes of the nation for further medals in the competition.

Note: Sometimes writers are not sure of the facts of the story that they are reporting and so, in order to avoid legal problems, they use vague phrases such as *It is believed that …, It is feared that …, It is claimed that …, He alleges that … .*

They may also use the **passive voice** to avoid reporting who was responsible for an action, or if they do not know who was responsible. For example: *A pedestrian was knocked down in High Street yesterday afternoon.*

EXERCISE 5.4

Choose one of the following news items and rewrite it to make it more interesting. You can use exaggeration, **direct speech** or try varying the opening sentences. You can also add adjectives and adverbs. Remember that news items tend to use the conventions of standard English – and you should too.

a In 2018 the Japanese tennis star Naomi Osaka defeated world champion Serena Williams to win her first grand slam title. She became the first Japanese Grand Slam singles champion. During the match there was an on-court dispute between Williams and the umpire which resulted in Williams receiving a penalty and being booed by the crowd. After the win, Osaka said that it was a little bittersweet and that it wasn't necessarily the happiest memory.

b The giant panda was one of the most endangered mammals on earth. Numbers are slowly increasing now thanks to successful conservation projects. Pandas faced extinction because of habitat loss. This occurred as a result of human developments. New protected reserves have therefore been created to provide the animals with a safe habitat. Chinese scientists say that this is proof that conservation methods can be successful.

Reading and writing

Sports reporting

> **Activity 5.5**
>
> Work in a pair. Read the following two reports aloud to each other. You will need to read ahead as you do this, so that your reading aloud makes sense. Now reread the following two reports carefully. The first report is taken from a newspaper in Australia and the second from a St Lucian newspaper.

Kyron McMaster wins the British Virgin Islands' first ever medal in perfect tribute to late coach

HURDLER Kyron McMaster paid tribute to his coach, who tragically died in Hurricane Irma, as he broke through to become the British Virgin Islands' first ever Commonwealth Games gold medallist.

KYRON McMaster had the message inked onto his arm, not that he needed any reminding of the coach to whom he was dedicating the British Virgin Islands first major international medal.

McMaster won the 400-meter hurdles gold medal at the Commonwealth Games on Thursday night, saying it was the first major medal of any kind for the British Virgin Islands.

One thing he got from Xavier 'Dag' Samuels in the seven years they worked together was guidance. So after Samuels died last year in Hurricane Irma that devastated their home country, McMaster had the word tattooed on to his left biceps.

He also wears a wristband with the word clearly marked on it on his right arm, just for reinforcement.

'Tonight the gold meant a lot to the country, but I did what my coach would have wanted me to, go out there and run

my race,' McMaster said. 'He's with me everywhere I go with the band and the tattoo on my arm.

'So today I came out here and had fun like he always would also tell me before my race – 'Enjoy the moment, don't pressure yourself in the race.'

McMaster posted three of the four fastest times in the grueling 400 hurdles in 2017, and was the only runner to go under 48 seconds in the season when he ran a 47.80 in Jamaica.

But he got nothing from the world championships in London, disqualified in his heat for running on the line that marked the limits of his lane. He put it behind him to close the season with a win in the IAAF's Diamond League in Zurich.

McMaster was never really threatened on the Gold Coast, winning in 48.25 from Jeffrey Gibson of the Bahamas and Jaheel Hyde of Jamaica.

'It's the first medal for the British Virgin Islands at any games so I'm pretty happy for that,' he said.

He said the world championships 'wasn't my time,' but he'd used it as motivation and moved on.

McMaster, who now trains at Clemson under coach Lennox Graham, also used the experience of surviving the hurricane as something to learn from. Life's short. 'For me it was coming to an experience and actually knowing not to take life for granted because at any moment stuff could happen, he said. 'For me to be in stuff like that, and then my coach, for me to come out here and do this today it shows a lot. Every opportunity go out there like it's your last.'

LEVERN SPENCER BRINGS ST LUCIA ITS FIRST GOLD MEDAL AT THE COMMONWEALTH GAMES

Liz-Anne De Beauville
April 14, 2018

Levern Spencer made all of St Lucia and the rest of the Caribbean proud in the wee hours of Saturday April 14th when she jumped 1.95m in the women's high jump, taking the top spot. The United Kingdom and Australia took the 2nd and 3rd spots respectively.

Her second attempt at the bar brought in St Lucia's very first gold medal at the 2018 Commonwealth Games. Adding to what is already a long list of accomplishments, with 2 bronze medals from the 2010 and 2014 Commonwealth Games, and her gold and bronze finishes during the 2015 and 2007 Pan Am Games, her performance at Gold Coast Australia continues to prove that the 33-year-old still has a lot to offer, and retirement may be a long way off.

▲ Gold medalist Levern Spencer of St Lucia

In an interview following her historic finish, Spencer said, 'It's a really good feeling and I am happy I'm the one making history for my country. In the last two editions of the Commonwealth Games I got bronze so I was determined to work hard this time to win gold and my results today were good enough.'

The Babonneau native, alongside team St Lucia, which includes Olympian Jeanelle Scheper who finished 9th in the women's high jump over the weekend, and the 2017 Sports Man of the Year, Albert Reynolds, have once again placed field events in the spotlight for St Lucia.

EXERCISE 5.5

1 What is the name of Kyron McMaster's late coach and who is his present coach?

2 Explain, using your own words, what McMaster means when he said that his coach is with him everywhere he goes. What is there about his appearance that reinforces this?

3 Why did McMaster say the World Championships 'wasn't my time'?

4 In what ways did Hurricane Irma influence McMaster's attitude to his event?

5 In how many Commonwealth Games in total has Levern Spencer won a medal?

6 Using your own words, give details of all that you have learned about the careers of Levern Spencer and of other athletes from St Lucia.

The two sports reports you have read are from the national newspapers of the athletes' home countries (the Virgin Islands and St Lucia). What similarities and differences can you find in the way the journalists:

- describe and give details about the athletes
- describe the competitions in which the two athletes won their gold medals
- write about both the athletes and the athletes' relationship to their home countries
- include features (such as quotations) to attract readers in the athletes' home countries
- vary their language to make it interesting (different sentence openers, mixture of direct and reported speech)?

Key skills

Bias

Do you remember?

KEY WORD

bias a particular feeling either for or against something, sometimes resulting from prejudice

Do you remember what **bias** is?

If journalists show bias, they may be prejudiced against someone for some reason, such as where they come from or their age. Or they may simply be a keen supporter of a sports team or a political party and so only present one point of view. Sometimes writers offer opinions without really being experts themselves. Read this example:

> The ageing Roger Federer took a while to get into the game while his more agile younger opponent rushed towards a first-set victory.

Using the word 'ageing' shows that the writer thinks Roger Federer is perhaps too old to be playing. To avoid bias, the writer could have said:

> The 41-year-old Roger Federer took a while to get into the game while his younger opponent rushed towards a first-set victory.

Now read this example:

> The basketball player, who is confined to a wheelchair, scored three goals.

The words 'confined to' show bias. To avoid bias, the writer could have said:

> The basketball player, who uses a wheelchair, scored three goals.

LET'S TALK

1 Do you think either of the articles you read are biased in any way? Give reasons for your answers.
2 Find an example of a biased news report and discuss why you think it is biased.

Activity 5.7

Work in a pair. You have been asked to write a news article about a local sports event.

1 Discuss the purpose of the article and the audience.
2 Then talk about how best you can organise and present it (PowerPoint, onscreen, social media or podcast, for example). What do you need to think about for each type of presentation?
3 Draft your article in your chosen format. Then edit and improve the article before you present it.

Reading

Reporting on the environment

HINT

As you read, think about how each writer develops ideas through the use of quotations from experts and other people. Which article uses a more human-interest perspective?

EXERCISE 5.6

Here are two reports from UK newspapers on the effects of global warming on ice at both the South and North Poles. Both were published at the end of 2019 and refer to events that took place in August of that year. The first is from the *Guardian* and the second from the *Daily Mirror*.

WORD ATTACK SKILLS

Work out from the context what these words mean:
- ✔ glacier
- ✔ ice shelf
- ✔ retrieve
- ✔ cavern
- ✔ autonomous
- ✔ pristine

Submarine to explore why Antarctic glacier is melting so quickly

Ian Sample, Science editor

An international team of scientists has reached the Thwaites **glacier** in Antarctica and is preparing to drill through more than half a kilometre of ice into the dark waters beneath.

The 600-metre deep borehole will allow researchers to lower down a torpedo-shaped robotic submarine that will explore the underside of the **ice shelf** to better understand why it is melting so fast. Thwaites glacier, which is part of the west Antarctic ice sheet, has lost an estimated 540bn tonnes of ice since the 1980s. But recent measurements show that the melting of the glacier is speeding up, sending even more ice into the Amundsen Sea.

'There are several glaciers in Antarctica that are doing similar things, but this is the one we are most worried about,' said David Vaughan, the director of science at the British Antarctic Survey, who has travelled south with the UK–US drilling team.

Thwaites glacier is one of the most remote and inhospitable places on Earth. It has taken the researchers weeks to get themselves and their equipment to the drilling site, a spot on the ice shelf about 1,500km (932 miles) from both the British Antarctic Survey's Rothera research station and the American McMurdo station.

In brutal conditions, where the temperature can fall below –20°C, the researchers will have only a few days to drill through the ice shelf, deploy the 'icefin' submarine and **retrieve** it, and set a suite of monitoring instruments into the ice before the hole freezes over. 'The aim is to do it as rapidly as possible. All of this will happen in three to four days. They really can't afford to muck about,' said Vaughan.

The expedition to the Florida-sized glacier became more pressing this year when Nasa scientists used ground-penetrating radar to reveal a massive cavity in its base. The **cavern**, two-thirds the size of Manhattan and 300 metres tall, was formed as 13bn tonnes of ice melted away over the past three years. The enormous cavity allows water to get under the glacier and melt it from beneath.

…

'Nobody has ever been able to drill through the ice close to where it starts to float and that is the critical point,' Vaughan told the Guardian. 'If everything goes to plan, they will drill the hole and then ream it out until it's about 50cm across, and then lower in the **autonomous** underwater vehicle. That will actually go into the cavity and send back images in real time so they can navigate it right up to the point where the ice starts to float.'

…

Thwaites glacier is already responsible for about 4% of the global sea level rise, as the ice slips off the land and into the sea. But because the ice shelf is melting and thinning, the glacier is speeding up.

Thwaites itself contains enough ice to raise global sea levels by more than 2 feet (61cm), but it holds back other inland glaciers that contain far more ice, enough to raise global sea levels by more than 2 metres.

'If Thwaites glacier melts, on its own, we will see a rise in sea level around our own coast,' said Vaughan. 'We are not saying that it's going to happen in the next 100 years or so, but it could certainly begin in that time period.'

KIDS PLAY IN ARCTIC SEAS AS 22°C HEATWAVE GRIPS NORTH POLE AT CLIMATE CHANGE FRONTLINE.

EXCLUSIVE: The Mirror reports from Greenland – the climate crisis front line – where 22°C temperatures are melting the ice at an unprecedented rate

By Nada Farhoud, Environment editor

A heatwave is gripping The Arctic, melting away Greenland's ice sheet on an unprecedented scale and threatening a global rise in sea levels – an urgent reminder of the climate crisis we are now all facing.

Kids splashing each other in the sea and locals wearing t-shirts were unheard of here in August 10 years ago.

…

Greenland, the world's largest island at almost three times the size of France, is now living with extreme environmental changes which could see the Arctic Sea free of ice by 2030 if no action is taken.

I travelled to Greenland, home to just 56,000 people, last week to see first-hand the drastic changes to conditions and to understand why it matters to us all.

Away from headlines about melting ice caps and pictures of underfed polar bears unable to stalk seals on flimsy ice forced to invade towns for food, I found a community battling to adjust.

Living alongside a backdrop of eerily beautiful icebergs and utterly terrifying melting sea ice and retreating glaciers is having a devastating impact on species, habitats and human life.

This is the frontline of climate change.

…

'If all of Greenland's ice were to melt, it would raise global sea levels by 6 metres meaning cities like London, Sydney and New York would be underwater and the whole of Bangladesh would disappear,' says Mark Wright, director of science at WWF, who accompanied the Daily Mirror to the Arctic.

'This is not science fiction. This is the reality of climate change.

'It is happening now – and here in accelerated terms – providing a crucial insight into what we will all face unless we urgently tackle this now.'

Sea ice now forms here two months later and melts one month earlier – as temperatures rise twice as fast as the global average.

This summer has seen more than 100 wildfires in the Arctic Circle devastating once pristine forests, turning them from precious carbon dioxide absorbing sponges into giant new emitters of greenhouse gases.

The country is also experiencing record-breaking temperatures. In mid-June, along the eastern coast it was 9°C warmer than the 1981–2010 average.

Just as western Europe has baked in a heatwave with record temperatures at the end of July, the hot air moved as far north as Greenland with the gauge hitting 22°C on August 1. The average high is around 7°C.

Perched beneath the world's second largest ice cap after Antarctica, nothing other than black moss and lichen grow here.

Fourth fifths of Greenland is buried under an ice sheet two miles thick, much of it three million years old.

But in the blink of an eye in geological terms it has begun melting – and much faster than climate change models predicted.

Around 60% is affected, including higher elevations that only rarely see temperatures climb above freezing.

In July alone 200 billion tonnes of meltwater poured into the Atlantic – enough to raise sea levels by 0.5mm.

We take a small fishing boat out with Joseph Manumina, 75, who points to a glacier he used to cross in a five-metre sled pulled by 16 huskies in the winter.

But like thousands of others here, the fourth-generation hunter has been forced to abandon his family trade and is now a fisherman.

Joseph stops his boat beside the Hiawatha glacier and points out when he was young it stretched hundreds of metres further into the fjord.

'The land you can now see was not visible at all a few years ago. But heavy rains came in 2016 and changed the landscape for good,' he said.

…

'What happens here will also affect what happens in the UK in terms of our weather patterns and security in coastal areas. This is why we have to take action and now', said Mark Wright, director of Science at WWF.

'We don't have long left to cap this rapid change that we've never seen before in human history.'

EXERCISE 5.7

1 Make a list of the facts that you learn from these articles about the melting of ice in the Antarctic and the Arctic, and the problems facing the people living in Greenland.

2 Using your own words as far as possible, explain what you learn from both articles about how the melting of ice at the Poles could affect the whole planet in the future.

KEY WORD

angle the point of view behind a writer's presentation of a topic

Putting a spin on things

The writer George Orwell said:

> A scrupulous writer, in every sentence that he writes, will ask himself at least four questions, thus: 1. What am I trying to say? 2. What words will express it? 3. What image or idiom will make it clearer? 4. Is this image fresh enough to have an effect?

This is pretty good advice for a writer, but it is also good advice for a politician!

Key skills

Political language

Politicians like to put a spin on what they say. They attempt to control their communication in order to deliver a particular message. To do this they choose their words carefully, often to put a positive 'spin' on events. For example:

> This is a proud day for us all!
>
> I am heartened by your magnificent support!

Here are some of the other ways in which politicians use language.

Active and passive voice

They use active and passive voices to give words more or less prominence.

The active voice is when the subject carries out the verb (for example, the president addressed the audience). This emphasises the subject or the person who carried out the action. The passive voice is when the subject is acted on by the verb (for example, the audience was addressed by the president). This emphasises whoever or whatever receives the action, or the action itself.

Look at the following three examples. How are they different?

> Minister of Finance announces tax hikes
>
> New tax hikes announced by Minister of Finance
>
> New tax cuts announced

Metaphors

Metaphors are widely used in political language. Very often the metaphors come from the language of war or conflict, or from sports. These metaphors help politicians to paint pictures of what they want us to believe. Sports images can make speeches seem less formal and more friendly.

Look at these examples. Can you suggest where these metaphors come from and what they mean?

> The gloves are off now. Let's win this.
>
> After a marathon campaign we finally have a winner.

Metonymy

Metonymy is a figure of speech in which a concept is referred to using a single name or term. For example, the President of the USA and the team of people who work with the President are often referred to as 'the White House'. (The White House is the President's official residence.) Do you know what each of these terms refers to?

> Number 10
>
> The Crown
>
> Hollywood

When used as a literary device, metonymy can add symbolism or deeper meaning to a piece of writing, drawing in the reader and grabbing their attention.

Personal pronouns

Politicians use pronouns such as 'you', 'your' and 'we' to make what they say more personal and to make us feel that we agree with them. They may say things such as:

> 'We are in this together.'
>
> 'We know what happened in the past.'
>
> 'You know what is right and what is wrong.'

EXERCISE 5.8

Read these sentences and explain the metaphors used in them.

1 You're on a sticky wicket now!
2 This new law will be a game changer for our country.
3 The politician tried to put a positive spin on the shocking events.
4 We will tackle this together.

Activity 5.8

Work in a pair. Read these short extracts from political speeches and discuss the political language used in them.

1 'We choose to go to the Moon. We choose to go to the Moon in this decade and do the other things, not because they are easy, but because they are hard, because that goal will serve to organize and measure the best of our energies and skills, because that challenge is one that we are willing to accept, one we are unwilling to postpone, and one which we intend to win, and the others, too.'
President John F. Kennedy, 1961, in a speech explaining why the USA would be sending a mission to land on the Moon

2 'There can be no doubt that this afternoon we are witnessing another historic advance in the struggle against discrimination in our society, this time against discrimination on grounds of sex. In introducing the Bill, I hope that there will be no difference between the two sides of the House about the principle. The only difference is that the present Government have had the will to act.'
The First Secretary of State and Secretary of State for Employment and Productivity (Barbara Castle), during a parliamentary session about a new law to guarantee women and men equal pay, 1970

In November 1854, during the Crimean War, a small force in the British army called the Light Brigade suffered an infamous military defeat. This event was one of the earliest battles to be reported by a war correspondent.

EXERCISE 5.9

Read this extract from the report about the conflict. Explain what picture the reporter, William Howard Russell, paints of the British troops through his choice of words. Is the text biased? Has the writer put a 'spin' on the information?

At 11:00 our Light Cavalry Brigade rushed to the front … The Russians opened on them with guns from the redoubts on the right, with volleys of musketry and rifles.

They swept proudly past, glittering in the morning sun in all the pride and splendour of war. We could hardly believe the evidence of our senses. Surely that handful of men were not going to charge an army in position? Alas! It was but too true – their desperate valour knew no bounds, and far indeed was it removed from its so-called better part – discretion. They advanced in two lines, quickening the pace as they closed towards the enemy.

> **DID YOU KNOW?**
> This report inspired the famous poem by Alfred, Lord Tennyson called 'The Charge of the Light Brigade'.

Politicians hold regular press conferences during which journalists ask them questions about their policies or about events. The press conferences are often carefully 'staged' and the questions and answers prepared in advance, but sometimes they are spontaneous as well.

Activity 5.9

Work in a group. You are going to role-play a press conference and then write a report about what you heard.

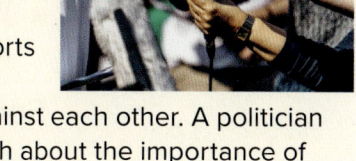

Imagine this scene. There is an important sports event in your country. Two teams of players from different places have arrived to play against each other. A politician arrives at the event and makes a short speech about the importance of the events. Some journalists interview the politician in a five-minute press conference.

As a group, decide who will be the politician. Discuss what the politician will say and how it will be said. Remember that you need to put a 'spin' on it. The politician may use the opportunity to brag about something he or she has done recently, unrelated to this sports event.

Then think of four or five tough questions to ask the politician.

HINT
Structure your report carefully:
- Introduction: Say what the report is about.
- Body: Describe the events to create human interest.
- Conclusion: Sum up and give your opinion. You can also make suggestions.

EXERCISE 5.10
Working alone, write a short news report (300–400 words) about the event using information from the press conference and some of the techniques you have explored in this unit. State your opinion about the interview clearly. Try to give your report a human-interest angle without introducing any bias.

SELF-CHECK
- Did you choose your words carefully?
- Did you include direct and indirect speech?
- Did you comment on what the politician said?
- Did you try to avoid bias?

Reviewing

Reflect on your learning in this chapter.

Reading

- What style of news do you like to read? Do you prefer to read tabloid stories, opinion columns or more serious pieces?
- How do you prefer to read articles: in newspapers, in magazines, online or another way? Why?
- Write a list of the skills and techniques you learned from reading and learning about reports.

Speaking and listening

- Did you work successfully as a group? Did you feel confident to contribute? What do you think you could improve?
- Did you learn anything by carefully listening to others?
- Do you find audio a useful medium via which to receive news (for example, on the radio, podcasts, online)? Why?

Writing

- What techniques did you use in your own reporting?
- Did you enjoy writing as a reporter? Why?

Key skills

- List up to five new words you have learned.
- Can you remember any of the language devices and their uses taught in this chapter?

Further reading

If you enjoyed reading these news articles, reflect on where you get your news and share some sites you enjoy with your friends and family.

Many news organisations, such as the *Guardian*, send daily updates free of charge if you subscribe – this can be a handy way of receiving daily news. Other organisations, such as the *Telegraph*, write newsletters on specific interests, such as their weekly women's sport newsletter.

FIVE-STAR REVIEWS

Reading
★ A descriptive piece for synonyms
★ Three articles about Bako National Park – comparison and contrast
★ Extracts to identify and understand irony
★ Humorous extracts using figures of speech

Speaking and listening
★ Taking part in a discussion about humour
★ Taking part in a discussion about sarcasm
★ Listening for sarcasm
★ Listening for humour

Writing
★ Summaries – note-taking methods
★ A letter providing key information
★ A playscript
★ A humorous memory, using hyperbole

Key skills
★ Homonyms, homophones, homographs, synonyms
★ Figures of speech
★ Planning, drafting and editing

LET'S TALK

Use these prompts to reflect on the topic of humour.

- What do you find funny?
- What films, TV programmes or videos make you laugh?
- Who is funny that you know? How do they make you laugh?
- What is the difference between humour and cruelty? Is humour ever cruel?
- How do you feel when people laugh at you?
- How do you feel if people don't laugh when you make a joke?

As a class, discuss the topic of humour.

Use your reflections on the prompts above to inform your contributions.

Listen and respond openly to different opinions and experiences.

Think carefully before you speak about how to describe your opinions without being insensitive to others.

Key skills

Vocabulary

Homonyms, homophones and homographs

The Greek **prefix** homo- means 'the same'. The exercises in this section are all based on groups of words that have similarities.

■ **Homonyms** are words that have the same spelling and pronunciation, but different meanings. For example, 'bit' can mean a small item of something and can be the past tense of the verb 'to bite'.

■ **Homophones** are words that have the same pronunciation, but different spellings and meanings, such as 'rain' (something wet that falls from the sky), 'rein' (a device for controlling a horse) and 'reign' (rule as king or queen).

■ **Homographs** are words that have the same spelling but different pronunciations and meanings, such as 'close', a verb meaning 'shut', and 'close', an adjective meaning 'near to'.

Being able to distinguish between words in these categories is important; you need to be able to do this in order to write and speak English fluently.

EXERCISE 6.1

The following words are homonyms – they each have at least two different meanings. Use each word in at least two different sentences that make their meanings clear:

bear   bow   fair   lap   lean   lie   page   pen   plain   train

EXERCISE 6.2

The following words are homophones. Use each of the pairs of words in sentences, making clear the differences in their meanings:

allowed / aloud   ascent / assent   bare / bear   berth / birth
cereal / serial   flair / flare   freeze / frieze   higher / hire
hoarse / horse   pedal / peddle

EXERCISE 6.3

The following words are homographs – they have a different meaning depending on how they are pronounced. Write two sentences for each word to illustrate their different meanings:

bow   desert   entrance   lead   live   minute   refuse   row
wind   wound

Choosing synonyms

The prefix syn-, derived from Greek language, means 'together'. This may help you remember that a **synonym** is a word or phrase that goes 'together' with another word or phrase because it has the same or a similar meaning.

A synonym is a word or phrase that means exactly or almost the same as another word or phrase in the same language, for example: small / tiny or hot / burning.

EXERCISE 6.4

In the extract below, the narrator describes his first impressions of an apparently deserted old house in the middle of a wood. Some words have been omitted. Select what you think are the best words to fill the gaps from the list of synonyms (1–10) below the extract:

Extract: *The House in the Mist*

The house, to which I now naturally directed a glance of much more careful …(1)… than before, was no ordinary farm-building, but a / an …(2)… old mansion, made conspicuously larger here and there by jutting porches and more than one convenient lean-to. Though furnished, warmed and lighted with candles, as I have previously described, it had about it an air of disuse which made me feel myself a / an …(3)…, in spite of the welcome I had received. But I was not in a position to stand upon ceremony, and ere long I found myself inside the great room and before the blazing logs whose …(4)… had lighted up the doorway and added its own attraction to the other allurements of the inviting place.

Though the open door made a …(5)… which was anything but pleasant, I did not feel like closing it, and was astonished to observe the effect of the mist through the square thus left open to the night. It was not an agreeable one, and, instinctively turning my back upon that quarter of the room, I let my eyes …(6)… over the wainscoted walls and the odd pieces of furniture which gave such an air of old-fashioned richness to the place. As nothing of the kind had ever fallen under my eyes before, I should have thoroughly enjoyed this opportunity of …(7)… my taste for the curious and the beautiful, if the quaint old chairs I saw standing about me on every side had not all been empty.

But the …(8)… of the place, so much more …(9)… than the solitude of the road I had left, struck cold to my heart, and I missed the cheer rightfully belonging to such attractive surroundings. Suddenly I bethought me of the many other apartments likely to be found in so spacious a dwelling, and, going to the nearest door, I opened it and called out for the master of the house. But only an echo came back, and, returning to the fire, I sat down before the cheering blaze, in quiet acceptance of a situation too lonely for comfort, yet not without a certain piquant interest for a man of free mind and …(10)… disposition like myself.

Anna Katherine Green

1   analysis, scrutiny, surveillance
2   confused, irregular, rambling
3   burglar, intruder, snooper
4   glare, glimmer, glow
5   breeze, draught, gust
6   ramble, roam, stray
7   appeasing, gratifying, obliging
8   detachment, retirement, solitude
9   depressing, disheartening, oppressive
10 adventurous, audacious, reckless

Reading and writing

Summarising from different texts

Writing a summary that takes information from more than one source is a slightly more challenging task. On these pages you will find three articles about Bako National Park in Borneo. Two of these articles are mainly factual, and one was written by a tourist who had visited the park. As you will see, some information is given in more than one article.

Read all three articles carefully and then do the exercises and activities that follow.

Extract: 'Introduction to Bako National Park'

With its rainforest, abundant wildlife, jungle streams, waterfalls, interesting plant life, secluded beaches and trekking trails, Bako National Park offers visitors an excellent introduction to the rainforest of Borneo. Bako may not have an instantly recognizable star attraction but there can be very few places in the world that pack so much natural beauty into such a limited area, all just 37 km from Kuching. Its accessibility – and its sheer range of attraction and activities – have made Bako one of the most popular parks in Sarawak.

Gazetted as a protected area in 1957, Bako is Sarawak's oldest national park, covering an area of 2742 hectares at the tip of the Muara Tebas peninsula. It is one of the smallest national parks in Sarawak, yet one of the most interesting, as it contains almost every type of vegetation found in Borneo. A well-maintained network of trails – from easy forest strolls to full-day jungle treks – allows visitors to get the most out of this unique environment.

www.bakonationalpark.com/bako-national-park-introduction-overview.php

---

Extract: 'What to see at Bako National Park'

The star of Bako National Park is undoubtedly the proboscis monkey, the big-nosed, pot-bellied comedian of the rainforest. But the star has a supporting cast of long-tailed macaque monkeys, usually patrolling the park headquarters, silvered leaf monkeys, monitor lizards and squirrels and flying lemurs that glide from tree to tree.

But why hurry? If you want to be sure of seeing the full cast of characters, stay overnight in one of the park's comfortable chalets with electricity and running water from a fresh mountain stream. There is also a cafeteria serving snacks and cold drinks, an education centre, a visitor room and an information centre.

You can see bearded pigs as you walk Bako's trails. Well used to human visitors, Bako's wildlife is less shy than their remote jungle cousins so you can get close enough to take photographs. Of course, you have an even better chance of experiencing Bako's biodiversity if you stay overnight at and take part in a night walk led by the park guides.

If birds are your interest, more than 190 species live at Bako, including some rare varieties. The birds and animals are easy to find along the 18 colour-coded walking trails that offer full-day jungle hikes to gentle strolls. The circular Lintang trail passes through all of Bako's vegetation types from dipterocarp forest, scrub-like padang, swamp forest, mangroves and delicate cliff vegetation. The Telok Delima and Telok Paku trails are the best vantage points for seeing proboscis monkeys in the early morning or late afternoon.

Small bays, steep cliffs and sandy beaches make Bako's coastline a delight. Along the sandy footpaths, you will find the insect-eating pitcher plants that have been known to devour small animals. From the beach at Pandan Kecil, you can see Bako's trademark, the rock formation called sea stacks, carved by the waves. For those who wish to enjoy quietness of nature, Lakei Island is a great place to go.

Bako's extensive trail system is made up of 16 colour-coded jungle trails which offer a range of walking and hiking options. The fit and adventurous can opt for full-day jungle hikes or overnight camping expeditions, whilst those who prefer to take it easy can opt for a relaxing forest walk.

www.sarawakforestry.com/parks-and-reserves/bako-national-park/

Extract: 'Getting there and accommodation'

A bus ride from Kuching to Bako Market takes about 45–60 minutes (red public bus number 1), originating from the wet market beside the Electra building, which will also pick up passengers from the burger stand opposite Riverside Majestic Hotel, Kuching and costs RM3.50 each way. Buses leave to/from Bako about once every hour starting from about 7am from Kuching and finishing about 6pm from Bako.

Minivans can be chartered for around RM30, and seat 5–7 people. They can reach Bako in half the time of the public bus, are stationed near the Open Air Market and depart when there are enough passengers.

When you arrive at the Bako Market right in front of the jetty/visitor center, register, purchase your entrance ticket and buy your boat ticket. This 20-minute boat ride will lead you to the Bako National Park Headquarters. Enquire at the registration counter for details.

Park accommodation consists of 3-bedroom chalets, 2-bedroom lodges, 4-bedroom hostels and a camping ground. Please contact the National Park Booking Office for the latest room rates reservations.

A permit is required for professional photography or filming, which should be arranged in advance with the National Park Booking Office.

www.sarawakforestry.com/parks-and-reserves/bako-national-park/

Compare, contrast and summarise

Activity 6.1

You have just read three different articles on the same subject.

Ask a partner to time you for two minutes as you make notes of as much as you can remember from the articles – think of the most appropriate way of taking notes quickly before you start.

When complete, share your remembered notes with a partner. Together, review the articles and fact-check your notes.

> **HINT**
> In the world of social media and internet news, *fact-checking* is an important skill. Rumours and falsehoods can spread very quickly – you should develop your fact-checking skills.
> - Read past the headline and look for the facts/evidence.
> - Check your source is reliable:
>   - Who wrote it? Who published it?
>   - Are other sources reporting or providing the same information?
> - Check the time and date the information was published.
> - Be aware of biased reporting.
> - Think before you share or use the information.

Activity 6.2

LET'S TALK

Read through the articles together. Look at the sentence openers and connectives.

Discuss how these sentence openers help the reader flow through the text and follow the connections.

Make a list of three useful sentence openers to use in your own writing.

The articles contain a mixture of facts, bias and opinions.

Work in a pair to collect notes under these headings:

Facts	Bias	Opinions

EXERCISE 6.5

Now work alone to write a brief summary of the articles as a bullet-point list of the five most important facts.

You will need to decide which facts you feel are the most important and which points are supplementary, and highlight the impact of any bias on the texts.

Writing and key skills

Writing a letter to provide information

EXERCISE 6.6

Imagine that you are part of a team organising a two-day visit to Bako National Park for your class at school. You have been asked to write a letter to parents explaining what there is to see and do at the park. Use details from the three articles that you have read and write 300–350 words.

> **KEY WORD**
>
> **author brief** this explains very clearly the purpose and form an author needs to use in a piece of written work. Professional authors are sent briefs as part of their contract. They must make sure they include all of the information and details required.

Here is the **author brief**:

- Audience: parents of the class
- Purpose: explain the educational value of the two-day trip to Bako National Park
- Content: describe the opportunities available, and explain how this is important for the education of the class
- Length: 300–350 words
- Form: formal letter

Follow this writing process:

- **Plan your letter**
  Work together with a partner. Decide on the number of paragraphs required, and the purpose of each paragraph.

- **Prepare your paragraphs**
  Write a draft sentence opener to begin each paragraph. The sentence opener should help the reader understand the flow of ideas and the purpose of each paragraph.

- **Write your letter**
  Write a first draft. Include details from what you have read, summarising facts as well as including details that will convince parents of the educational value of the trip.

- **Evaluate and edit**
  Work with your partner again. Swap letters. Read for accuracy and to check whether the writing has met the author brief. Give each other feedback in order to make improvements for a final draft.

Figures of speech – advanced techniques

Student's Book 7 looked at similes and metaphors. Here are some more figures of speech that you are likely to come across. You may find examples of them in newspapers.

Remember that although it is useful to know the names of the terms, merely spotting them (in poems in particular) is not enough to gain good marks in an examination. What is important is to be able to explain the effects that writers achieve by using them.

Oxymoron

An **oxymoron** is a figure of speech that combines two normally contradictory terms to create a special effect. For example:

> deafening silence
>
> bitter sweet

Paradox

A **paradox** is similar to an oxymoron. It is a situation or statement that seems impossible because it contains two contradictory facts. For example:

> The child is father to the man.

Litotes

Litotes is the term used for understatement. To use litotes, you say what something is, by explaining that it is not the opposite.

> Cabbage stew is not my favourite dinner.

In other words, Cabbage stew? Yuck!

Hyperbole

Hyperbole is deliberate exaggeration for effect and is, therefore, the opposite of litotes. For example:

> The queue for the cinema was miles and miles long.

Climax

A **climax** is a list, very often consisting of three elements, in which each element intensifies the statement made by the previous one, until the last one provides the final hammer blow. For example:

> I expect to hear the truth, the whole truth and nothing but the truth.

Anticlimax or bathos

An **anticlimax** or **bathos** is, of course, the opposite of a climax. Here the final element in a list is in sudden contrast with the others, which either makes the elements that came before seem less serious or (less commonly) makes them seem more serious. For example:

KEY WORDS

oxymoron a figure of speech that combines two normally contradictory terms to create a special effect
paradox a situation or statement that seems impossible because it contains two contradictory facts
thyperbole deliberate exaggeration
climax a list, often consisting of three elements, in which each element intensifies the statement made by the previous one
anticlimax/bathos the final element in a list that trivialises the seriousness of the preceding elements

---

> In moments of crisis I size up the situation in a flash, set my teeth, contract my muscles, take a firm grip on myself and, without a tremor, always do the wrong thing.
>
> *George Bernard Shaw*

Irony

Irony is a particularly effective literary device and is a feature of many English novels, particularly those written in earlier times. At its simplest it is very similar to sarcasm as an ironic comment means exactly the opposite of what it appears to say. For example:

> We're having an absolutely wonderful time over here.

In other words, we're bored out of our minds.

Activity 6.3

Read through these descriptions and examples with a partner.

1 Try to think of another example of each figure of speech. Write them on pieces of paper to be shared with the class. Pass these around and try to decide which figure of speech they are examples of.

2 Ask your teacher to suggest where you can carry out research to find other examples of these figures of speech. Collect as many examples as you can for use in your own writing.

3 As a class, share the results of your research. Display your favourite examples for everyone to use in their own writing.

Speaking and listening

Using irony and humour to make a serious point

Sarcasm is a type of irony. It is when you say one thing, but you make it clear you mean the exact opposite.

Sarcasm can be used for humour, but it can also be used to make people feel small.

Look at these examples:

Oh you're *so* funny!

That was *so* interesting.

I can't *wait* to hear all about it.

HINT

Remember that, within your group, points of view and feelings may differ. Listen and respond politely. Respect one another's opinions.

Activity 6.4

Discuss these examples and others with the class. Read them aloud to one another, placing the emphasis in the correct place. How does it sound? Has anyone ever been sarcastic to you? How does it feel? Is there a right time and place for sarcasm?

Using irony for effect

Although irony is similar to sarcasm, it can be far more subtle and effective. Here is an extract from the beginning of Charles Dickens' *Hard Times*. One of Dickens' aims in this book is to attack the nineteenth-century educational belief that all that children need to be taught are facts and practical details.

In this extract, Thomas Gradgrind, the owner of the school, and a government school inspector are questioning a class of children. Among them are Sissy Jupe (whose father is a horse trainer in a circus) and Bitzer, whose head is full of 'bits' of facts. Each is asked to define a horse. The irony of the situation is that Sissy, who has lived with horses all her life, isn't able to do this, whereas Bitzer (who lives in a town and has little experience of horses) gives an answer that meets the inspector's requirements. Dickens' use of irony highlights the limitations of the educational system. (The extract has been slightly edited.)

GLOSSARY

breaks horses – trains horses to be ridden in the circus ring; sometimes trained to perform tricks

farrier – puts shoes on horses

behoof – interest

pitchers – jugs (the pupils are seen as jugs to be filled with facts)

quadruped – four-legged creature

graminivorous – eats grass

grinders, eye-teeth, incisive – types of teeth

sheds – loses a covering, such as hair

shod with iron – given shoes made of iron

Extract: *Hard Times*

'Girl number twenty,' said Mr Gradgrind, squarely pointing with his square forefinger, 'I don't know that girl. Who is that girl?'

'Sissy Jupe, sir,' explained number twenty, blushing, standing up, and curtseying.

'Sissy is not a name,' said Mr Gradgrind. 'Don't call yourself Sissy. Call yourself Cecilia.'

'It's father as calls me Sissy, sir,' returned the young girl in a trembling voice, and with another curtsey.

'Then he has no business to do it,' said Mr Gradgrind. 'Tell him he mustn't. Cecilia Jupe. Let me see. What is your father?'

'He belongs to the horse-riding, if you please, sir.'

Mr Gradgrind frowned, and waved off the objectionable calling with his hand.

'We don't want to know anything about that, here. You mustn't tell us about that, here. Your father **breaks horses**, don't he?'

'If you please, sir, when they can get any to break, they do break horses in the ring, sir.'

'You mustn't tell us about the ring, here. Very well, then. Describe your father as a horsebreaker. He doctors sick horses, I dare say?'

'Oh yes, sir.'

'Very well, then. He is a veterinary surgeon, a **farrier**, and horsebreaker. Give me your definition of a horse.'

(Sissy Jupe is thrown into the greatest alarm by this demand.)

'Girl number twenty unable to define a horse!' said Mr Gradgrind, for the general **behoof** of all the little **pitchers**. 'Girl number twenty possessed of no facts, in reference to one of the commonest of animals! Some boy's definition of a horse. Bitzer, yours.'

…

'Bitzer,' said Thomas Gradgrind. 'Your definition of a horse.'

'**Quadruped. Graminivorous.** Forty teeth, namely twenty-four **grinders**, four **eye-teeth**, and twelve **incisive. Sheds** coat in the spring; in marshy countries, sheds hoofs, too. Hoofs hard, but requiring to be **shod with iron**. Age known by marks in mouth.' Thus (and much more) Bitzer.

'Now girl number twenty,' said Mr Gradgrind. 'You know what a horse is.'

Charles Dickens

Activity 6.5

1   Discuss the use of irony in the extract. What do you think Dickens *actually* believes education should be like?
2   Use evidence from the text to show how Charles Dickens uses humour to make the reader understand that although the characters are saying one thing, in fact the *author* has a different message.
3   Explain, including evidence from the text, how Dickens shows the different personalities of:
    ◾ Gradgrind
    ◾ Sissy
    ◾ Bitzer.

EXTENSION

There is a lot of skilfully written dialogue in this extract. One way of enjoying it and bringing it fully to life is to rewrite it as a playscript and act it out in class.

Create a playscript of the extract, with the main characters. Decide on how to perform the dialogue so that the audience understands the silliness of the points.

Do you remember?

Remember irony is a literary technique that writers use to criticise something. They do this by describing the thing in such a way that an alert reader realises that they actually mean the opposite of the words they use or the situation that they are presenting.

Reading and speaking

Humour in personal writing

We have practised summarising texts and reducing what was written to its key points. The ability to select and edit material is an important life skill and something that you will need to practise.

In the extract that follows, the American novelist Edith Wharton recounts a motoring tour that she made in England with her friend Henry James, another American novelist. The two writers are uncertain of their route and stop the car to ask a man in the street for directions. James spoke, as he wrote, in long, complex sentences using formal and grandiose vocabulary. The **prolixity** of this question is very effectively countered by the answer it receives! (If you don't know what 'prolixity' means, read the extract then have a guess before you look it up.) You may want to think about this **anecdote** when someone asks you why it is important to learn how to write summaries!

Extract: 'Where is ...?'

'My good man, if you'll be good enough to come here, please; a little nearer – so,' and as the old man came up: 'My friend, to put it to you in two words, this lady and I have just arrived here from Slough; that is to say, to be more strictly accurate, we have recently passed through Slough on our way here, having actually motored to Windsor from Rye, which was our point of departure; and the darkness having overtaken us, we should **be much obliged** if you would tell us where we now are in relation, say, to the High Street, which, as you of course know, leads to the Castle, after leaving on the left hand the turn down to the railway station.'

I was not surprised to have this extraordinary appeal met by silence, and a dazed expression on the old wrinkled face at the window; nor to have James go on: 'In short' (his **invariable prelude** to a fresh series of **explanatory ramifications**), 'in short, my good man, what I want to put to you in a word is this: supposing we have already (as I have reason to think we have) driven past the turn down to the railway station (which in that case, by the way, would probably not have been on our left hand, but on our right) where are we now in relation to …'

'Oh, please,' I interrupted, feeling myself utterly unable to sit through another **parenthesis**, 'do ask him where the King's Road is.'

Edith Wharton

KEY WORD

anecdote a short recount of an event, usually humorous or interesting

Activity 6.6

Take it in turns to read parts of the extract out to the group. Notice how long each sentence is, and how deep a breath you have to take before you begin!

EXERCISE 6.7

Here is the complete question that Henry James asked the old man in the street. Translate it into your own words and remove any details that you think are not relevant.

> 'My friend, to put it to you in two words, this lady and I have just arrived here from Slough; that is to say, to be more strictly accurate, we have recently passed through Slough on our way here, having actually motored to Windsor from Rye, which was our point of departure; and the darkness having overtaken us, we should be much obliged if you would tell us where we now are in relation, say, to the High Street, which, as you of course know, leads to the Castle, after leaving on the left hand the turn down to the railway station. In short, my good man, what I want to put to you in a word is this: supposing we have already (as I have reason to think we have) driven past the turn down to the railway station (which in that case, by the way, would probably not have been on our left hand, but on our right) where are we now in relation to … Ah –? The King's Road? Just so! Quite right! Can you, as a matter of fact, my good man, tell us where, in relation to our present position, the King's Road exactly is?'

EXERCISE 6.8

Edith Wharton is making a humorous point about Henry James's style of speech and writing:

It takes him a long time to get to the point!

Here are some very simple questions.

Is it going to rain today?  What's for dinner?

Are we nearly there yet?  Did you remember your sports kit?

Activity 6.7

Share your Jamesian sentences with the class.

Read them aloud – practise first so that your tone matches the style of the language.

Have a go at pretending to be Henry James (who is considered one of the very greatest writers of English!).

Turn these questions and answers into Jamesian style.

Make them as long and rambling as you can.

WORD ATTACK SKILLS

Find the following words in the text:

- ✔ misleading
- ✔ frantic
- ✔ gastric disorder
- ✔ unyielding
- ✔ unopposed
- ✔ distressed
- ✔ bickering
- ✔ painstakingly

Predict their meaning from the text, then check your answers by using a dictionary or an online dictionary recommended by your teacher.

Write the correct definition for each word.

Activity 6.8

With a partner:

- ■ answer the following questions:
  - ■ How did the extract make you feel?
  - ■ Did you find it funny? Why/why not?
- ■ find quotations that show how Bill Bryson has used in humour in his writing.

Reading and writing

Humour in non-fiction

In the following extract from his **autobiography** *The Life and Times of the Thunderbolt Kid*, Bill Bryson writes about a game that was popular when he was growing up in the USA in the 1950s. Read this extract carefully and then do the exercise that follows.

Extract: *The Life and Times of the Thunderbolt Kid*

However, the worst toy of the decade, possibly the worst toy ever built, was electric football. Electric football was a game that all boys were compelled to accept as a Christmas present at some point in the 1950s. It consisted of a box with the usual exciting and totally **misleading** illustrations containing a tinny metal board, about the size of a breakfast tray, painted to look like an American football pitch. This vibrated intensely when switched on, making twenty-two little men move around in a curiously stiff and **frantic** fashion. It took ages to set up each play because the men were so fiddly and kept falling over, and because you argued continuously with your opponent about what formations were legal and who got to position the last man, since clearly there was an advantage in waiting till the last possible instant and then abruptly moving your running back* out to the sidelines where there were no defenders to trouble him. All this always ended in bitter arguments, punctuated by reaching across and knocking over your opponent's favourite players, sometimes repeatedly, with a flicked finger.

It hardly mattered how they were set up because electric football players never went in the direction intended. In practice what happened was that half the players instantly fell over and lay twitching violently as if suffering from some extreme **gastric disorder**, while the others streamed off in as many different directions as there were upright players, before eventually clumping together in a corner, where they pushed against the **unyielding** sides like victims of a nightclub fire at a locked exit. The one exception to this was the running back who just trembled in place for five or six minutes, then slowly turned and went on an **unopposed** glide towards the wrong end zone until knocked over with a finger on the two-yard line by his **distressed** manager, occasioning more **bickering**. At this point you switched off the power, righted all the fallen men, and **painstakingly** repeated the setting-up process.

* a player position in American football

Bill Bryson

Writing and speaking

Presenting a humorous piece of nostalgia

Nostalgia is remembering the past or past events with fondness or longing; for instance, if somebody has moved away from home, eating or smelling a meal native to their home city or country could make them feel nostalgic. Nostalgia can also evoke sadness; for instance, an adult remembering happy days at school and knowing they won't be returning again as a student may make them feel sad about the reality of growing older, even though the memories are happy.

Activity 6.9

Bill Bryson describes his experiences humorously and in a strongly individual way. The challenge in summarising the extract is to separate facts about the game from his descriptions of it.

Re-read the extract and write a very brief summary (100–150 words) in which you explain the:

■ facts: what electric football was and how it was played
■ opinions: what Bill Bryson disliked about the game.

Share your work with a partner or small group and compare your findings: did you all agree on which parts were fact and which were opinion?

Using hyperbole for effect

Bill Bryson uses hyperbole – exaggeration – all the way through his article.

Activity 6.10

1 Find and copy five different examples of hyperbole from Extract: *The Life and Times of the Thunderbolt Kid* and explain why they are exaggerations.
Share your findings with the class.
Discuss their comic effect.

2 Think about a similar context from your childhood.
Did you have a toy that never worked properly? Or perhaps a family tradition that was supposed to be fun but that always ended in arguments? Were you ever taken on a trip or outing that was supposed to be fun but turned out to be tremendously dull?

3 You are going to write a short speech about the memory – using hyperbole throughout. You do not need to be cruel or unkind, but should simply use hyperbole to bring humour to the memory.

Share your ideas with a partner, and use the following brief:

■ Describe the event or object clearly – the listeners may not know anything about it.
■ Use hyperbole for a humorous effect.

4 When you have written a first draft, read it aloud to your partner. Talk about the balance of fact and humour. Does the humour take over? Do you need to reduce the amount of hyperbole?

5 Present your speech to the whole class.
If appropriate, you could use visual prompts or even a slideshow to provide the audience with context.
Think about the simple visual prompts that would help your listeners to understand the context of your speech.

Reading

Reading for pleasure and understanding

David Mitchell is a British comedian, actor, writer and television presenter. He writes a regular opinion column for a UK Sunday newspaper in which he at times confronts some of the more unusual aspects of modern life.

In the article that follows he questions how anyone can claim that something can be considered the very best of its type in the world. The article has been slightly abridged.

Guinness World Records is on a slippery slope

A street in Wales has replaced one in New Zealand as being the world's steepest. How long until another road claims the title?

The world has a new steepest street! But it's more than 1,000 years old. So, did something happen to the previous steepest street? Is this an **off-colour** attempt to look on the bright side of a horrendous natural disaster? No, the previous steepest street is still there.

So, has the old one somehow got less steep, perhaps because of a horrendous natural disaster? No, it's as steep as ever. There is no horrendous natural disaster involved with this story. So what's happened?

Well, a street has been discovered that's steeper than the street that, for some years, has been proclaiming itself to be the world's steepest street. But how can a street be discovered? Was it buried? Is it part of a newly unearthed hilly suburb of Pompeii? No, stop trying to link it to horrendous natural disasters.

The new steepest street has been in continuous occupation since **time immemorial**. Much longer, in fact, than its **predecessor** as holder of the **accolade**. So, the fact is – and I hate to be rude about what we now know is, at best, the second steepest street in the world – that this predecessor was an **impostor**, a **usurper**, albeit an unknowing

one. It was never steepest. Even on the day of its construction, a steeper street already existed.

Fundamentally, this is a damning **indictment** of the system by which the title of world's steepest street is awarded, a process that, slightly suspiciously, appears to have something to do with Guinness.

It turns out, you see, that when a street claims to be the steepest in the world, Guinness World Records is rigorous about the evidence of the street's existence and precise steepness that must be provided. So when the **advocates** of Baldwin Street in Dunedin, New Zealand, (until recently proclaimed the world's steepest street) said it had a gradient of 35%, that assertion was carefully verified as was the fact that it is genuinely a street rather than a random strip of mountainside devoid of **asphalt** or dwellings.

Where the rigour lapsed, however, was in failing to check whether there were any other streets that were steeper. It's a strange lapse, when you think about it. It seems so obvious: in order to know which is the world's steepest street, you need to measure the steepness of every street in the world.

Now, you may say that that is one hell of a **logistical** challenge. Who's going to pay for that to be done? And the wearying expense and difficulty is, to my mind, only **compounded** by the undeniable truth that finding out which of the world's millions of streets happens to be steepest is a colossally unimportant task. I would have been content with a state of affairs where everyone agreed that Baldwin Street in Dunedin is certainly jolly steep, and probably a lot steeper than most streets, and we left it at that.

→

The problem came in choosing to elevate that undeniable status to 'world's steepest street' without knowing how steep all the other ones were. It's a strange mistake for a records organisation to make. You'd think that Guinness World Records, of all institutions, would be well aware that a person or thing being very [insert adjective] does not make it particularly likely that they are the most [insert adjective] in the entire world.

The tallest bloke you've ever met is almost certainly not the tallest man on Earth. He might be, but you really have to check. You can't just watch him fetch a football off a garage roof, say 'Wow' and then stick it in your book – not if you think that being accurate about these records matters. Personally, I don't think it matters, but I'd expect the people running Guinness World Records to think it does if they want to cling on to an **iota of professional pride** and aren't just in it for all the free Guinness they probably no longer get.

There are other people it seems to matter to as well because, bizarrely, being named the world's steepest street actually generates a bit of tourism. Some people want to go and see the world's steepest street. More people than want to avoid it. I don't really understand why. Steep is a bad thing for a street to be. Streets are supposed to **facilitate** access to houses or shops. The steeper it is, the less well it does that. It would be like being the street with the worst maintained road surface in the world or being littered with the greatest density of **impacted** chewing gum.

Nevertheless, there is genuinely a small amount of sadness in Dunedin that Baldwin Street has lost its status and a small amount of joy in Harlech in Wales that a very old street there, called Ffordd Pen Llech (which looks like more of a lane if you ask me), has been confirmed as always having been steeper.

But how long can that joy last when the majority of the world's street gradients remain unmeasured and unverified? What a **precarious** position: constantly worrying about losing the title if another street proves it's in a more precarious position.

David Mitchell

WORD ATTACK SKILLS

Find the following words in the text:

- ✔ off-colour
- ✔ time immemorial
- ✔ predecessor
- ✔ accolade
- ✔ impostor
- ✔ usurper
- ✔ indictment
- ✔ advocates
- ✔ asphalt
- ✔ logistical
- ✔ compounded
- ✔ iota of professional pride
- ✔ facilitate
- ✔ impacted
- ✔ precarious

Predict their meaning from the text, then check your answers by using a dictionary or an online dictionary.

EXERCISE 6.9

1   Using your own words and referring closely to the extract, explain the argument that David Mitchell is making in this article.

2   By looking closely at his use of language in this article (in particular the repetition of vocabulary, the similes and metaphors), explain how the writer conveys his attitude towards his subject.

EXTENSION

There are many world records. Some are inspiring. Some are terrifying, and some are silly.

Ask your teacher to recommend a suitable way to read about a range of world records.

Find a particular example that captures your attention. It could be humorous, inspiring or revolting. The important aspect is that you have a strong personal response.

Write an article to convey both the facts and your personal response. Use the techniques you have learned to plan and present your article, so that it would be suitable for your school newspaper or website.

Reviewing

Reflect on your learning in this chapter.

Reading

- Comparing multiple texts can be challenging. How did you find the Bako National Park comparison task?
- Which of the texts in this chapter did you most enjoy reading? Why?
- What did you think of Bill Bryson's style? Would you like to read more of his book?
- Write a list of the techniques you learned from one or more of the authors in Chapter 6.

Speaking and listening

- How do you feel about reading aloud to your class? Have you grown in confidence?
- During group work, did you feel able to contribute to the discussion?
- Did speaking in, and listening to, sarcastic tones make you feel a certain way? Has it changed your opinion about the use of sarcasm, or how people talk to one another?
- Did it help to work with others when planning your own writing?

Writing

- What techniques did you use in your own writing?
- You need to be decisive and succinct when identifying and summarising key points. How did you find the summary task?
- Did you enjoy inserting humour into your writing? Why?

Key skills

- Was it useful to learn about figures of speech? Why?
- List up to five new words you have learned.
- List three pairs of synonyms and three pairs of homonyms.

Further reading

If you enjoyed reading these humorous extracts, you might enjoy:

- *Charming but Insane* by Sue Limb
- *Big Bones* by Laura Dockrill
- *Boys Don't Knit* by T.S. Easton
- *Bollywood Babes* by Narinder Dhami
- *The Hitchhiker's Guide to the Galaxy* by Douglas Adams
- *Spud* by John van de Ruit
- *Henry Tumour* by Anthony McGowan

7 Interesting characters

Reading
★ Limericks and poems
★ Identifying voice in fiction and poetry
★ Identifying the rhyming schemes in sonnets

Speaking and listening
★ Taking part in a discussion about your favourite poems and authors
★ Using your voice and body language to role-play a character
★ Discussing literary devices

INTERESTING CHARACTERS

Writing
★ A nonsense poem
★ A comparative analysis of two poems

Key skills
★ Using quotations from a text to support your answers
★ Comparing and analysing two poems
★ Comparing poems from the same poet

LET'S TALK

Readers make choices about the poems and stories they read and they respond in different ways.

> I like action and adventure! It's like an escape for me. It makes me switch off from everyday routines.

> I like to read stories and poems that make me laugh ... and think! They make me relax.

Which types of characters do you like in poems or stories? Humorous characters? Characters to whom you can relate (feel close)?

How do you choose which poems or stories to read?

Do you read poems and stories written by different authors or do you go back to the same authors? Why?

A limerick is a humorous poem of just five lines. The first, second and fifth lines end with words that rhyme with each other, and have seven to ten syllables and the same rhythm. The third and fourth lines have five to seven syllables and the same rhythm; they also end in words that rhyme with each other.

HINT

Make sure your limerick **scans** properly. You must have the correct number of stressed syllables in each line (unless you are making a point, as in the second limerick you read).

KEY WORD

scans a poem scans when it follows a regular pattern of stressed and unstressed syllables

GLOSSARY

lark, wren – types of birds

Reading and speaking

Interesting characters in poems

Poet: Edward Lear

Edward Lear (1812-88) was an English artist, illustrator, musician, author and poet. He is best known for his nonsense poems, especially limericks, which he made popular with readers and other poets who have since copied the format.

Activity 7.1

Work with a partner.

1 Read the following two limericks aloud. To do this you need to find the rhythm, so decide which syllables need to be stressed. Try reading the limericks aloud in different ways to see what works best. Discuss which words the poet has used to create the rhythm in each limerick. What is the intended effect of this rhythm?

2 Which limerick do you like best? Why? Discuss this with a few other pairs of learners too.

3 Discuss the characters described in each limerick.

4 Then write your own nonsense limerick about an imaginary character. You can write this by hand or present it onscreen, whatever works best. Read it to others in the class and get their feedback.

'There Was an Old Man with a Beard'

There was an Old Man with a beard,
Who said, 'It is just as I feared! –
Two Owls and a Hen,
Four **Larks** and a **Wren**,
Have all built their nests in my beard.'

Edward Lear

'There Was a Young Bard of Japan'

There was a Young **Bard** of Japan,

Whose limericks never would scan;

When told it was so,

He said: 'Yes I know,

But I always try and get as many words into the last line as I possibly can.'

Anonymous

Spotlight on: rhyming couplets

A rhyming couplet is two lines in a poem, usually of the same length, that rhyme and have the same **meter**. The lines follow each other and together make up one thought.

Activity 7.2

Work in a small group.

1   Read the following poem which describes an imaginary character, the Snitterjipe. It is written in rhyming couplets. Take turns to read each couplet aloud, reading ahead so that you get a feel for the meter and the rhymes.

2   Discuss the poem:
   ■   What does the Snitterjipe look like? Could you draw a picture of it from the description?
   ■   Why were the boys afraid? What could they see, hear and feel?
   ■   What literary devices does the poet use in this poem? Think about alliteration, assonance and hyperbole, for example. To what effect does the poet use these?

3   Make up another rhyming couplet that could add to the description of this creature. Share your couplet with the rest of the class.

KEY WORD

meter the pattern of stressed and unstressed syllables in a poem

Writer: James Reeves

John Morris Reeves (1909–78) was a British writer who wrote poetry, stories and plays for adults and children.

'The Snitterjipe'

In mellow orchards, rich and ripe,
Is found the luminous Snitterjipe.
Bad boys who climb the bulging trees
Feel his sharp breath about their knees;
His trembling whiskers tickle so,
They squeak and squeal till they let go.
They hear his far-from-friendly bark;
They see his eyeballs in the dark
Shining and shifting in their sockets
As round and big as pears in pockets.
They feel his hot and wrinkly hide;
They see his nostril flaming wide,
His tapering teeth, his jutting jaws,
His tongue, his tail, his twenty claws.
His hairy shadow in the moon,

It makes them sweat, it makes them swoon;
And as they climb the orchard wall,
They let their pilfered **pippins** fall.
The Snitterjipe suspends pursuit
And falls upon the fallen fruit;
And while they flee the monster fierce,
Apples, not boys, his **talons** pierce.
With thumping hearts they hear him munch –
Six apples at a time he'll crunch.
At length he falls asleep, and they
On tiptoe take their homeward way.
But long before the blackbirds **pipe**
To welcome day, the Snitterjipe
Has fled afar, and on the green
Only his fearsome prints are seen.

James Reeves

WORD ATTACK SKILLS
Word out the meanings of the following words from clues in the poem:
✔   pippins (noun)
✔   talons (noun)
✔   pipe (verb)

Interesting characters in novels

Author: Lewis Carroll

Charles Lutwidge Dodgson (1832-98), who is better known by his pseudonym (the name is used as an author), Lewis Carroll, was an English writer noted for his clever use of words and creation of nonsense literature. *Alice's Adventures in Wonderland* and its sequel *Through the Looking-Glass* are his most well-known works.

Alice's Adventures in Wonderland tells the story of a seven-year-old girl named Alice, who falls through a rabbit hole into an underground fantasy world populated by strange creatures. She shrinks and grows in size during the adventure as a result of eating and drinking various things.

Spotlight on: writer's voice

A writer's voice is the way a writer chooses to tell a story. This involves using a variety of techniques such as narration (for example, **first** or **third person**) and dialogue, and making careful choices about the words to use and the way sentences are constructed.

KEY WORDS

first-person narration uses 'I', gives a personal view

third-person narration refers to characters as he / she / they or by name; is less personal than first-person narration and is sometimes anonymous, but often gives opinions

Activity 7.3

Read the following short extracts from *Alice's Adventures in Wonderland*, by Lewis Carroll. As you read, make notes or think about what each scene reveals about the characters. How does the writer's voice help to create each character?

Discuss and answer these questions:

1   Who is the narrator? What does the narrator tell us or suggest to us about the characters? Does this influence your idea of the characters?

2   How has the writer used dialogue to tell us about the characters?

3   Lewis Carroll said that Alice was 'loving and gentle', 'courteous to all', 'trustful' and 'wildly curious'. Do you agree? Give reasons for your answers.

4   Write up character notes for each character. You will use these when you act out the scenes from the book.
    Here are some adjectives that may be useful:

curious	polite	innocent	confused	courageous	cheeky
superior	condescending	wise	bizarre	well-mannered	
argumentative	bold	self-centred	clever	intimidating	

5   Act out each scene in your group, taking turns to act different roles. Use the character notes you have written. Use your voices and body language to help create the characters.

WORD ATTACK SKILLS

Work out the meaning of the following words from the context of the extract:
✔   languid
✔   contemptuously

Extract: *Alice's Adventures in Wonderland*

The Caterpillar and Alice looked at each other for some time in silence: at last the Caterpillar … addressed her in a **languid**, sleepy voice:

'Who are *you*?' said the Caterpillar.

This was not an encouraging opening for a conversation. Alice replied, rather shyly, 'I – I hardly know, sir, just at present – at least I know who I was when I got up this morning, but I think I must have changed several times since then.'

'What do you mean by that?' said the Caterpillar sternly. 'Explain yourself!'

'I can't explain myself, I'm afraid, sir,' said Alice, 'because I'm not myself, you see.'

'I don't see,' said the Caterpillar.

'I'm afraid I can't put it more clearly,' Alice replied very politely, 'for I can't understand it myself to begin with; and being so many different sizes in a day is very confusing.'

'It isn't,' said the Caterpillar.

'Well, perhaps you haven't found it so yet,' said Alice; 'but when you have to turn into a chrysalis – you will some day you know – and then after that into a butterfly, I should think you'll feel it a little queer, won't you?'

'Not a bit,' said the Caterpillar.

'Well perhaps your feelings may be very different,' said Alice; 'all I know is, it would feel queer to *me*.'

'You!' said the Caterpillar **contemptuously**. 'Who are *you*?'

Which brought them back again to the beginning of the conversation. Alice felt a little irritated at the Caterpillar's making such very short remarks, and she drew herself up and said, very gravely, 'I think you ought to tell me who *you* are, first.'

'Why?' said the Caterpillar.

Here was another puzzling question; and as Alice could not think of any good reason, and as the Caterpillar seemed to be in a very unpleasant state of mind, she turned away.

'Come back!' the Caterpillar called after her. 'I've something important to say!'

This sounded promising, certainly: Alice turned and came back again.

'Keep your temper,' said the Caterpillar.

'Is that all?' said Alice, swallowing down her anger as well as she could.

'No,' said the Caterpillar.

…

Later she meets the Cheshire Cat sitting in a tree.

The Cat only grinned when it saw Alice. It looked good-natured, she thought; still it had very long claws and a great many teeth, so she felt that it ought to be treated with respect.

'Cheshire Puss,' she began, rather timidly, as she did not know whether it would like the name; however it only grinned a little wider. 'Come, it's pleased so far,' thought Alice, and she went on. 'Would you tell me, please, which way I ought to go from here?'

'That depends a good deal on where you want to get to,' said the Cat.

'I don't much care where –' said Alice.

'Then it doesn't matter which way you go,' said the Cat.

'– as long as I get *somewhere*,' Alice added as an explanation.

'Oh, you're sure to do that,' said the Cat, 'if you only walk long enough.'

Alice felt that this could not be denied, so she tried another question. 'What sort of people live about here?'

'In *that* direction,' the Cat said, waving its right paw round, 'lives a Hatter; and in that direction,' waving the other paw, 'lives a March Hare. Visit either you like: they are both mad.'

'But I don't want to go among mad people,' Alice remarked.

'Oh, you can't help that,' said the Cat; 'we're all mad here. I'm mad. You're mad.'

'How do you know I am mad?' said Alice.

'You must be,' said the Cat, 'or you wouldn't have come here.'

Lewis Carroll

Author: J.R.R. Tolkien

J.R.R. Tolkien was an English writer, poet and academic, best known as the author of the fantasy works *The Hobbit* and *The Lord of the Rings*.

He created a memorable imaginary character called Gollum who appeared in *The Hobbit* and *The Lord of the Rings*. In the extract you will read, a hobbit called Bilbo Baggins meets Gollum for the first time.

EXERCISE 7.1

Read the extract from *The Hobbit* and then write your answers to these questions:

1 What is your impression of Gollum from the description in this extract? Write one sentence in your own words to describe what you think he is like.

2 How was Bilbo feeling when Gollum saw him? Quote words from the extract to support your ideas.

3 Why does Gollum suggest that they play a game of riddles? Give two possible reasons.

4 Comment on the way that Gollum speaks.
   a Who is Gollum speaking to when he says: 'What iss he, my preciouss?'
   b Find three examples of non-standard English that he uses.
   c Why is 'preciouss' written with more than one 's'?

5 Look at the role of the narrator in this extract.
   a Who do you think narrates the first paragraph? What makes you think this?
   b When does the narration change to the third person? Why do you think the author does this?

GLOSSARY
flummoxed – confused, not understanding

Extract: *The Hobbit*

Deep down in the dark water lived old Gollum, a small slimy creature. I don't know where he came from, nor who or what he was. He was Gollum – as dark as darkness, except for two round pale eyes in his thin face. He had a little boat, and he rowed about quite openly on the lake; for lake it was, wide and deep and deadly cold. He paddled it with large feet dangling over the side, but never a ripple did he make. Not he. He was looking out of his pale lamp-like eyes for blind fish, which he grabbed with his long fingers, quick as thinking.

…

Gollum got into his boat and shot off from the island, while Bilbo was sitting on the brink altogether **flummoxed** and at the end of his way and his wits. Suddenly up came Gollum and whispered and hissed:

'Bless us and splash us, my preciousss! I guess it's a choice feast; at least a tasty morsel it'd make us, Gollum!' And when he said *gollum* he made a horrible swallowing noise in his throat. That is how he got his name, though he always called himself 'my precious'.

The hobbit jumped nearly out of his skin when the hiss came to his ears, and he suddenly saw the pale eyes sticking out at him.

'Who are you?' he said, thrusting his dagger in front of him.

'What iss he, my preciouss?' whispered Gollum (who always spoke to himself through never having anyone else to speak to). This is what he had come to find out, for he was not really hungry at the moment, only curious; otherwise he would have grabbed first and whispered afterwards.

'I am Mr Bilbo Baggins. I have lost the dwarves and I have lost the wizard, and I don't know where I am; and I don't want to know, if only I can get away.'

'What's he got in his handses?' said Gollum, looking at the sword, which he did not quite like.

'A sword, a blade which came out of Gondolin.'

'Ssss,' said Gollum, and became quite polite. 'Praps ye sits here and chats with it a bitsy, my preciousss. It likes riddles praps it does, does it?' He was anxious to appear friendly, at any rate for the moment, and until he found out more about the sword and the hobbit, whether he was quite alone really, whether he was good to eat, and whether Gollum was really hungry. Riddles were all he could think of. Asking them, and sometimes guessing them, had been the only game he had ever played with other funny creatures sitting in their holes in the long, long ago before he lost all his friends and was driven away, alone, and crept down, down, into the dark under the mountains.

'Very well,' said Bilbo, who was anxious to agree, until he found out more about the creature, whether he was quite alone, whether he was fierce or hungry, and whether he was a friend of the goblins.

'You ask first,' he said, because he had not had time to think of a riddle.

So Gollum hissed:

What has roots as nobody sees,

Is taller than trees.

Up, up it goes,

And it never grows?

J.R.R. Tolkien

HINT

Think about the dialogues (direct speech), for example the short responses from the Caterpillar, the straightforward answers from Bilbo and the questions that Alice asks.

KEY WORD

foil someone or something that makes another person's good or bad qualities more noticeable

LET'S TALK

1 Talk about the characters in the extracts you have read. What techniques did each author use to create the characters for their readers?
2 Which character did you enjoy the most? Why?
3 Do you think that Alice's character provides a **foil** for the other eccentric characters she meets in Wonderland? And what about Bilbo and Gollum?

Activity 7.4

Work in a pair. Act out the scene between Gollum and Bilbo. Express what you have learned about each character in your body language and in the way you speak the part. You can make up some of your own words too.

How can acting out a scene help you to understand a character better?

Free verse is a poetic form that does not have a regular meter or rhythm. It does not rhyme, or if it does, there is no fixed form or pattern. Poets use free verse to give their own shape and meaning to a poem. They may, however, use other poetic devices, such as metaphors or alliteration, to add meaning or effects to their poem. They may also use punctuation creatively.

Different voices

EXERCISE 7.2

The following short poem was written by a learner and is written in free verse. Read the poem by yourself and answer the questions.

1 Explain in your own words what the poem is about.

2 Explain the images the poet uses to describe what the speaker looks like and how effective they are in adding meaning to the poem.

3 Comment on the **voice** in the poem.

4 Do you think the speaker has a positive or a negative self-image? Give a reason for your answer.

KEY WORD

voice the voice is the speaker in a poem (like a narrator in a story)

'The Photo Shoot'

Enveloped in soft silk I stand

Majestic, I turn my face into the cool breeze

Of the electric fan blowing my hair into ribbons of fire

ONE … POSE … TWO … CLICK

The bright white flash turns me into a molten swirl of colour

I am a fantasy of human artwork

I can be anything you want me to be

I look into the shiny lens and see my future flash before me.

Alison Pitout (Wynberg Girls High School)

Poet: Grace Nichols

Grace Nichols was born in Guyana, in South America, and later emigrated to the United Kingdom. Her award-winning collections of poetry are popular with adults and children. Her poetry is influenced by Guyanese and Amerindian folklore and the Caribbean culture in which she grew up.

DID YOU KNOW?

A praise song is a traditional poetic form from Africa which praises leaders, family members, friends, animals, plants and places. It is meant to be sung or chanted.

Activity 7.5

Work in a pair.

1 Read the poem 'Praise Song for My Mother' silently to get an idea of what it is about. Summarise this in one sentence.

2 Discuss and work out the meanings of the words in the Word Attack Skills box. If you are not sure about any of them, use a dictionary. The words are all **present participles**.

3 Discuss these questions about the form and literary devices used in this poem:

a Explain why this poem is an example of free verse.

b Describe the voice in the poem.

c The poem uses metaphors to convey deeper meaning. For example, in the first **stanza** the author uses water as a metaphor to explain what her mother meant to her. She describes her mother as 'deep and bold and fathoming', like water. To 'fathom' means to work out or measure the depth of water. So, perhaps the poet is suggesting that her mother could always work out her deeper feelings? Look at the next three stanzas and work out the metaphors used in each and how they add to the meaning.

d Comment on the repetition and lack of punctuation in the poem. What effect does this have? Does it add to the meaning? (Hint: Read the poem aloud.)

e Why do you think the poet used the past tense in the lines 'You were'?

f What does the last line suggest? How important is this to the poet?

KEY WORDS

present participle a word formed from a verb ending in '-ing', used as an adjective or to form a verb tense

stanza a verse in a poem which is made up of two or more lines, which often have a common rhyme and pattern

WORD ATTACK SKILLS

Work out the meaning of the following words from the context of the poem:

✔ fathoming
✔ mantling
✔ streaming
✔ replenishing

GLOSSARY

gill – the organ of the fish that allows it to breathe under water

flame tree – a tree with bright red flowers, common in tropical countries

plantain – a fruit that looks like a banana, usually fried and eaten

'Praise Song for My Mother'

You were
water to me
deep and bold and **fathoming**

You were
moon's eye to me
pull and grained and **mantling**

You were
sunrise to me
rise and warm and **streaming**

You were
the fish's red **gill** to me
the **flame trees** spread to me
the crab's leg/the fried **plantain** smell **replenishing** replenishing

Go to your wide futures, you said

Grace Nichols

Dramatic dialogue

Poet: Langston Hughes

Langston Hughes was an American poet, social activist, novelist, playwright and columnist from Missouri in the United States of America. He became the leader of the Harlem Renaissance which was an intellectual and cultural revival of African American music, dance, art, fashion, literature, theatre and politics in the 1920s and 1930s.

KEY WORDS

persona a role or character taken on by a writer

extended metaphor an implied comparison that is continued over several lines or paragraphs in writing

symbolism using symbols to suggest ideas and qualities

Spotlight on: dramatic monologue

A dramatic monologue is a poem written in the form of a speech, spoken by one character with the reader being the audience. The poet takes on the voice of a character or a fictional identity (the **persona**) and reveals their feelings, inner thoughts and motivations.

Activity 7.6

Read the poem 'Mother to Son' and then discuss and answer these questions:

1 If someone asked you what this poem was about, what would you say – in one sentence?
2 What advice does the mother give her son? Why?
3 What sort of language does the poet use? Is it formal, informal, standard English? Why do you think the poet uses this language?
4 The poet uses an **extended metaphor** in the poem. What two things is he comparing? Find the words that create this implied comparison.
5 Why does the poet use short sentences? What effect does this have?
6 What does the staircase **symbolise** in the mother's life?

'Mother to Son'

Well, son, I'll tell you:
Life for me ain't been no crystal stair.
It's had tacks in it,
And splinters,
And boards torn up,
And places with no carpet on the floor –
Bare.
But all the time
I'se been a-climbin' on,
And reachin' landin's,
And turnin' corners,
And sometimes goin' in the dark
Where there ain't been no light.
So boy, don't you turn back.
Don't you set down on the steps
'Cause you finds it's kinder hard.
Don't you fall now –
For I'se still goin', honey,
I'se still climbin',
And life for me ain't been no crystal stair.

Langston Hughes

Listening and reading

Sonnets

Spotlight on: sonnets

Sonnets often cover such themes as love, jealousy, beauty and mortality and they are often written about a person or about a relationship with a person.

A sonnet is a poem made up of 14 lines with a specific **rhyme scheme** and meter. It originated in Italy in the thirteenth century. There are three main types of sonnet:

- The Italian (or Petrarchan) sonnet (Petrarch was a fourteenth-century Italian poet) uses only four or five different rhymes in its 14 lines. The rhymes are in a set pattern, with that of the first eight lines (known as the octave) being ABBA ABBA and that of the next six (the sestet) being either CDC CDC or CDE CDE.
- The English (or Shakespearean) sonnet also uses 14 lines, but comprises three groups of four lines each (known as quatrains) and a final couplet consisting of two lines. The usual pattern of the rhyme scheme is ABAB CDCD EFEF GG.
- The Spenserian sonnet, used by the sixteenth-century English poet Edmund Spenser, is a variation on the Shakespearean sonnet, and follows the rhyming pattern ABAB BCBC CDCD EE.

The first example is a Petrarchan sonnet by Elizabeth Barrett Browning.

Activity 7.7

1 Listen to the following sonnets as you read along. Discuss what they are about. Who are the characters described? What are the themes?

2 Compare the rhyme schemes of the sonnets, using A B C D to show the pattern. Your teacher will give you copies of the sonnets.

'How Do I Love Thee?'

How do I love thee? Let me count the ways.
I love thee to the depth and breadth and height
My soul can reach, when feeling out of sight
For the ends of being and ideal grace.
I love thee to the level of every day's
Most quiet need, by sun and candle-light.
I love thee freely, as men strive for right.
I love thee purely, as they turn from praise.
I love thee with the passion put to use
In my old griefs, and with my childhood's faith.
I love thee with a love I seemed to lose
With my lost saints. I love thee with the breath,
Smiles, tears, of all my life; and, if God choose,
I shall but love thee better after death.

Elizabeth Barrett Browning

And here is a Shakespearean sonnet:

Sonnet 130

My mistress' eyes are nothing like the sun;
Coral is far more red than her lips' red;
If snow be white, why then her breasts are dun;
If hairs be wires, black wires grow on her head.
I have seen roses damask'd, red and white,
But no such roses see I in her cheeks;
And in some perfumes is there more delight
Than in the breath that from my mistress reeks.
I love to hear her speak, yet well I know
That music hath a far more pleasing sound;
I grant I never saw a goddess go;
My mistress, when she walks, treads on the ground:
And yet, by heaven, I think my love as rare
As any she belied with false compare.

William Shakespeare

EXERCISE 7.3

1   The poem below is a sonnet written using the Shakespearean form. The first and fourteenth lines are in the right order but the lines in the middle have been mixed up. Using your understanding of the rhyming pattern of this form of poetry, rearrange the lines into the correct order.

Idea 61: Since there's no help, come let us kiss and part

Now at the last gasp of Love's latest breath
Shake hands for ever, cancel all our vows,
When, his pulse failing, Passion speechless lies;
Nay, I have done, you get no more of me;
Be it not seen in either of our brows
Now, if thou wouldst, when all have given him over
And I am glad, yea glad with all my heart,
When Faith is kneeling by his bed of death,
And when we meet at any time again,
And Innocence is closing up his eyes –
That we one jot of former love retain.
That thus so cleanly I myself can free.
From death to life thou might'st him yet recover!

Michael Drayton

2   Write a few sentences in which you explain briefly what the sonnet is about.

3   When do you think this sonnet might have been written? At the time Shakespeare wrote his sonnets (the sixteenth/seventeenth century) or more recently? What makes you think this?

Key skills

Comparing poems by the same poet

Think about why you find one book or poem more enjoyable than another, and the particular qualities that are the reasons for your choice. Once you start to do this, you are developing the technique of analysis – instead of just saying 'I like this poem' you are moving on to saying, 'I like this poem *because …*'.

How do you do this? Focus on the similarities and differences in the:
- form (type of poem)
- use of language
- choice of subject matter (theme).

Activity 7.8

1   Work in a group and read the following poem by Robert Frost, 'Mending Wall'.
2   Discuss what the poem is about:
- Who are the characters in the poem?
- What is the setting?
- How does the poet develop the characters? What do they do and say that helps us understand them?

WORD ATTACK SKILLS

Work out the meaning of the following words from the context of the poem:
- abreast
- mending-time
- boulders
- notion

'Mending Wall'

Something there is that doesn't love a wall,
That sends the frozen-ground-swell under it,
And spills the upper boulders in the sun;
And makes gaps even two can pass abreast.
The work of hunters is another thing:
I have come after them and made repair
Where they have left not one stone on a stone,
But they would have the rabbit out of hiding,
To please the yelping dogs. The gaps I mean,
No one has seen them made or heard them made,
But at spring mending-time we find them there.
I let my neighbor know beyond the hill;
And on a day we meet to walk the line
And set the wall between us once again.
We keep the wall between us as we go.
To each the boulders that have fallen to each.
And some are loaves and some so nearly balls
We have to use a spell to make them balance:

'Stay where you are until our backs are turned!'

We wear our fingers rough with handling them.

Oh, just another kind of out-door game,

One on a side. It comes to little more:

There where it is we do not need the wall:

He is all pine and I am apple orchard.

My apple trees will never get across

And eat the cones under his pines, I tell him.

He only says, 'Good fences make good neighbors.'

Spring is the mischief in me, and I wonder

If I could put a notion in his head:

'Why do they make good neighbors? Isn't it

Where there are cows? But here there are no cows.

Before I built a wall I'd ask to know

What I was walling in or walling out,

And to whom I was like to give offense.

Something there is that doesn't love a wall,

That wants it down.' I could say 'Elves' to him,

But it's not elves exactly, and I'd rather

He said it for himself. I see him there

Bringing a stone grasped firmly by the top

In each hand, like an old-stone savage armed.

He moves in darkness as it seems to me,

Not of woods only and the shade of trees.

He will not go behind his father's saying,

And he likes having thought of it so well

He says again, 'Good fences make good neighbors.'

Robert Frost

EXERCISE 7.4

1 Listen to another poem by Robert Frost on audio. You may remember this poem from Stage 7. Your teacher will give you a copy of the poem after you have listened to it.

2 Make some notes to compare the poems:
   - Is the form the same?
   - Is the language the same?
   - Are the themes the same or related in any way?
   - Is the voice of the poet the same?

LET'S TALK

Share and discuss your notes with your group.

Writing

Written analysis and comparison

It will become increasingly important during your studies to be able to analyse a piece of writing and compare its qualities with those of another piece of writing about a similar topic or written in a similar genre.

Writing an analytical comparison of two poems

1 Begin your comparison with an introductory paragraph in which you refer to the main points of similarity between the poems. Refer to the titles of the poems. Similarities could be in:
   - subject matter (for example, both poems are about characters)
   - poetic form (for example, both poems use the sonnet form, both poems are odes)
   - the date of composition (for example, both poems were written in the nineteenth century).

   Remember that acknowledging differences and ways in which the poems contrast with each other should also be mentioned.

2 The next step is to identify the speaker of the poem – in some poems it is clear that the poet is speaking in their own voice but in others (dramatic monologues, for example) the poet may be using a persona and speaking in the voice of a character. Once you have identified who is speaking the poem, then you should make some general comments about the speaker's attitude, feelings, etc.

3 Consider the mood and overall tone of the poem – for example, is it sad, upbeat, reflective? How does the poet convey this? Through poetic devices, word choice, rhythm, punctuation? Remember to consider how the poem supports your comments and include appropriate textual references and quotations.

4 Paraphrase the poem verse by verse, ensuring that you make clear your understanding of the meanings of the lines.

5 In your conclusion, you should consider the overall theme of the poem and especially how its specific details contribute to a universal meaning which relates to people of different generations and circumstances. Remember that in a comparison of two poems, the considerations in your conclusion should draw together the points of similarity and difference between them.

Here are two poems for you to compare: 'The Darkling Thrush' and 'A Blackbird Singing'.

1 Read them both carefully. When you have gained a general idea of what the poets are saying, read through the notes that your teacher will give you. These notes will help you understand the poems more fully.

2 Read and then write a comparative analysis of the two poems. In particular, you should consider the treatment of the subject matter and how the writers combine structural, linguistic and literary features for effect.

GLOSSARY

darkling – in the dark

coppice – a small group of trees growing closely together

bine-stems – long, flexible twining stem of a plant

lyres – old type of stringed instrument

outleant – laid out

crypt tomb, burial place

fervourless – lacking all feeling and passion

illimited – unrestrained

carolings – singing of carols

terrestrial – relating to the earth

nigh – near

'The Darkling Thrush'

I leant upon a coppice gate
        When Frost was spectre-grey,
And Winter's dregs made desolate
        The weakening eye of day.
The tangled bine-stems scored the sky
        Like strings of broken lyres,
And all mankind that haunted nigh
        Had sought their household fires.

The land's sharp features seemed to be
        The Century's corpse outleant,
His crypt the cloudy canopy,
        The wind his death-lament.
The ancient pulse of germ and birth
        Was shrunken hard and dry,
And every spirit upon earth
        Seemed fervourless as I.

At once a voice arose among
        The bleak twigs overhead
In a full-hearted evensong
        Of joy illimited;
An aged thrush, frail, gaunt, and small,
        In blast-beruffled plume,
Had chosen thus to fling his soul
        Upon the growing gloom.

So little cause for carolings
        Of such ecstatic sound
Was written on terrestrial things
        Afar or nigh around,
That I could think there trembled through
        His happy good-night air
Some blessed Hope, whereof he knew
        And I was unaware.

Thomas Hardy

GLOSSARY

ore – natural rock that contains valuable minerals

overtones – something suggested rather than stated

HINT

Remember, use each writing task to develop your handwriting. Over time your handwriting should become easier to read and easier to write: keep track of this by comparing your current handwriting with previous writing tasks and note any areas for improvement. Keep your handwriting in a flowing style.

'A Blackbird Singing'

It seems wrong that out of this bird,
Black, bold, a suggestion of dark
Places about it, there yet should come
Such rich music, as though the notes'
Ore were changed to a rare metal
At one touch of that bright bill.

You have heard it often, alone at your desk
In a green April, your mind drawn
Away from its work by sweet disturbance
Of the mild evening outside your room.

A slow singer, but loading each phrase
With history's overtones, love, joy
And grief learned by his dark tribe
In other orchards and passed on
Instinctively as they are now,
But fresh always with new tears.

R.S. Thomas

Reviewing

Reflect on your learning in this chapter.

Reading

- Which of the poems did you prefer?
- Would you read any of the poems again, or choose to read more from a particular poet?
- Did you enjoy the extracts from the novels *The Hobbit* and *Alice's Adventures in Wonderland*? Would you like to read either of the books in full? Why or why not?
- Which character from the extracts was your favourite and why?
- How do you feel about reading aloud? Has your confidence or opinion about this changed since the beginning of the school year?

Speaking and listening

- Performing a role play can be a daunting task. How did you approach this?
- Did you memorise some of the lines? Did you use body language and tone to portray your character?
- Do you think you worked well as part of a small group or with a partner? What do you think you could improve?

Writing

- Did you enjoy writing a nonsense poem? Do you prefer writing with a humorous or serious tone? Why?
- How did you approach the comparative analysis of two poems exercise? Did you find any aspects of this challenging?

Key skills

- List up to five new words you have learned.
- What other key skills have you learned from Chapter 7?

Further reading

If you enjoyed reading these extracts, you might enjoy:
- *Poems to Live your Life By* by Chris Riddell
- *A Poem for Every Night of the Year* by Allie Esiri
- *Alice's Adventures in Wonderland* by Lewis Carroll
- *Passport to Here and There* by Grace Nichols
- *Selected Poems* by Langston Hughes

THE FUTURE OF ENGLISH

Reading
- ★ An extract from The British Isles (Old English)
- ★ An extract from *The Canterbury Tales*
- ★ An extract from *Beowulf*
- ★ Poetry: 'Sir Gawain and the Green Knight' (Middle English)

Speaking and listening
- ★ Taking part in a discussion about English
- ★ Dialect – listening to and speaking in dialect
- ★ Taking part in a discussion about a character

Writing
- ★ A brief report about languages
- ★ A summary about Old English
- ★ An alliterative poem
- ★ Using rhyming couplets
- ★ A translation

Key skills
- ★ Inflected language
- ★ Dialect
- ★ Word origins
- ★ Research

LET'S TALK

Discuss these questions as a class:
- ■ When did you first learn English? Do you feel you are still learning English?
- ■ What do you think are the best ways to learn a language?

Speaking and writing

The development of English

The population of the world is approaching 8 billion (8,000,000,000) people. As a rough estimate, there are about 7,000 different languages spoken around the globe, with about 200 languages having 1 million or more speakers.

> **Spotlight on: English**
>
> The most commonly spoken language is Mandarin Chinese, which has over 900 million native speakers (people who have spoken the language since they were young children). English is the third most commonly spoken language in the world, with about 370 million native speakers (approximately 5 per cent of the world's population).

English is spoken far more widely than any other language and, particularly through the influence of the internet, is spreading significantly. Throughout the world, 55 countries (from Antigua to Zimbabwe) have English as an official language and in a further 53 countries English is widely understood by a large number of the population.

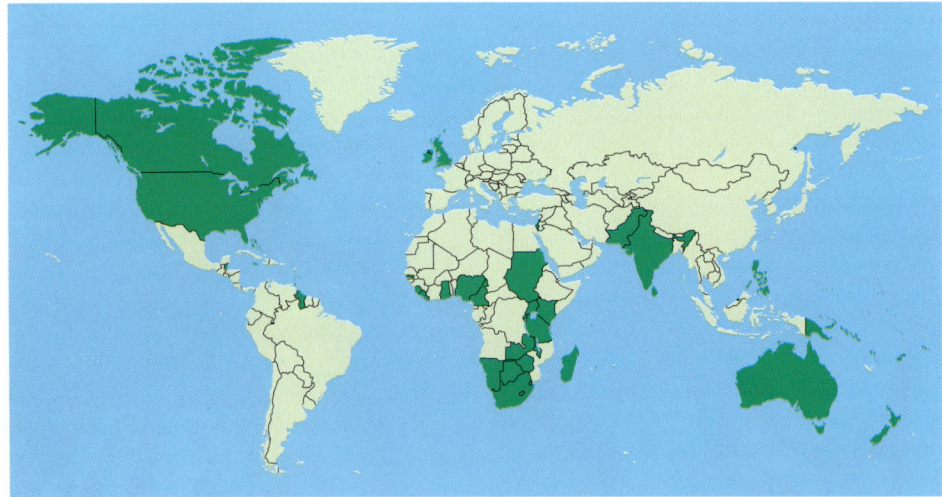

▲ The shaded areas show the countries in which English is an official language.

Activity 8.1

Recall the answers that were given during the Let's Talk class discussion, and build on those by working in a group to research and answer the following:

1 What languages are spoken in the country where you live? Do you, your friends and your family speak different languages?
2 Is English a main language in the country where you live?
3 In your life, when is English spoken or heard most often?

KEY WORD

factual information information that is accurate and true. This can be found in texts such as textbooks, encyclopedias, recipes and timetables

EXERCISE 8.1

Work alone to write a brief report about one of the languages spoken in the country where you live.

Give **factual information** such as the number of speakers, the main uses of the language, and any historical details you can find.

In this chapter we are going to look at the story of English – where it came from, how it developed and the different types of English spoken around the world.

Reading

Old English

EXERCISE 8.2

Read the text below and answer the questions that follow.

An introduction to Old English

The original inhabitants of the British Isles were the Celts, who (not surprisingly) spoke a language called Celtic (pronounced *keltic*). About 2,000 years ago, the Romans conquered England and established themselves as rulers there. Although they had a great influence on the infrastructure of British society, building roads and forts, for example, they rarely used the Celtic language and continued to speak Latin among themselves. The Celts continued to speak Celtic to each other.

About 1,500 years ago, Britain was invaded (and settled) by tribes from mainland Europe (from the area that is now Germany). These tribes were known as the Angles, Saxons and Jutes, and they spoke various dialects of a Germanic language. When they settled in mainland Britain, they, naturally, brought their language with them.

Over time, the language of the Germanic tribes became established as the main language spoken in what is now England. It is referred to as Old English or Anglo-Saxon.

During the eighth and ninth centuries, Britain was subjected to raids by people from Scandinavia (known as Vikings, from the Old English word 'wicing', which meant 'pirate'). The Vikings spoke a language known as Old Norse, and as a result many Old Norse words became absorbed into Old English.

1 Who lived in the British Isles at the time of the Roman conquerors?

2 Explain why the Romans may have had difficulty communicating with the inhabitants of Britain.

3 Find the word 'infrastructure' in the text. Use the context of the sentence to predict the meaning of the word, and then research it fully using a dictionary.

   Write a full definition of the word.

4 Find the bracketed phrase '(not surprisingly)' in the middle of one sentence.

   Explain its meaning in the context of the sentence. Include your interpretation of why the writer would choose to use brackets here.

5 Find four different examples of sentence openers in the text that help the reader understand how the text moves through time.

6 Write a brief summary of how Old English became 'established as the main language', and how it was influenced by Vikings.

> **EXTENSION**
>
> The Celtic language did not vanish. There remained Celtic speakers in Scotland, Wales, Ireland and even parts of mainland Europe.
>
> Research some of the modern languages of the world that are related to Celtic.
>
> Write a report to present to your class on this subject.

Key skills and writing

Old English – an inflected language

Modern Standard English retains just a few aspects of being an **inflected** language. This means some words change depending on which part of the sentence they are. For example, pronouns in English change depending on if they are the:

- subject: the person or thing performing the action of the verb

or

- object: the person or thing that the verb acts on.

In English, the subject nearly always appears *before* the main verb, and the object very often appears *after* the main verb.

EXERCISE 8.3

1   Identify the main verb, the subject and the object in each sentence:
    a   The Celts traded with the Romans.
    b   Over 1,000 years ago, tribes from Europe invaded Britain.
    c   While in Britain, the Romans built roads, forts and other structures.
    d   The history of English goes back to the Anglo-Saxons.

2   Copy and underline the pronouns used in each sentence below. Indicate whether they are the subject or the object, then rewrite the sentences using the correct form of each pronoun.
    a   Shyly, he gave the present to she and her smiled with a little embarrassment.
    b   Although his normally calm, my father lost he temper before demanding that us stop arguing and help he with the cooking.
    c   I had been rather lonesome until them was the first people to be friends with I when me arrived in this school.
    d   Although she brother didn't like to be seen with she, nevertheless she was very fond of he.

3   Copy the table and put the pronouns in the correct column. Some pronouns may appear in both columns.

| he   I   we   she   him   it   you   they   her |

Used as the subject	Used as the object

4   Choose the correct form of the verb 'to be' in each of these sentences. Write the sentences in Standard English.
    a   I be / are / am / is sorry for being late.
    b   She be / are / am / is next in the queue.
    c   They be / are / am / is unlikely to wait for much longer.
    d   He be / are / am / is often unhappy with the food.
    e   We be / are / am / is just delighted to be able to see the performance.
    f   You be / are / am / is certainly not alone.
    g   It be / are / am / is going to rain for many days.

KEY WORD

inflected Old English, or Anglo-Saxon, is an inflected language. In Old English, the endings of nouns change to indicate which case they are (subject, object, possessive, etc.) and the endings of verbs also change depending on whether they are first, second or third person, singular or plural. Many modern languages are inflected, such as German, French and Spanish.

EXTENSION

Modern English commonly uses the order 'subject-verb-object' to show the parts of the sentence.

We often define the subject as the person or thing that performs the action of the verb.

Work with a partner. What do you think the subject refers to in each sentence?

It is raining.

It is Wednesday the day after tomorrow.

It never fails to surprise me when you're late for class.

All is forgiven.

Reading

Old English: *Beowulf*

Many examples of written Old English still survive, such as the epic poem *Beowulf* and the historical Anglo-Saxon Chronicle, which was written by monks over several centuries. You can find readings of Beowulf in Old English online if you search using the key words "Beowulf Reading in Old English". Listen along and see if you can recognise any words.

This extract is taken from the Anglo-Saxon epic poem *Beowulf*. It tells of the adventures of the great hero Beowulf, a man of great strength, and of his battles against monsters and a dragon. This part of the story is set in the palace of Heorot, the court of Hrothgar, the King of Denmark, which is repeatedly attacked by the monster Grendel. Beowulf and his men are waiting within Heorot for Grendel to attack. This extract describes the monster making its way towards them.

EXERCISE 8.4

Read the original text, and then read the translation.

Compare the translation with the original version. How many words can you find that are similar to their modern English equivalents?

Make a list of pairs of words you think are equivalent.

HINT

The poem was composed anonymously, possibly at some time during the eighth century, but not written down until later.

The poem would have been declaimed – spoken loudly and with a strong rhythm – by a performer, and passed from person to person through memory.

Try to bring some of this strength to your performance.

Extract: *Beowulf*

Ða com of more   under misthleoþum

Grendel gongan,   godes yrre bær;

mynte se manscaða   manna cynnes

sumne besyrwan   in sele þam hean.

Wod under wolcnum   to þæs þe he winreced,

goldsele gumena,   gearwost wisse,

fættum fahne.   Ne wæs þæt forma sið

þæt he Hroþgares   ham gesohte;

næfre he on aldordagum   ær ne siþðan

heardran hæle,   healðegnas fand.

Translation

Then, from off the moor, under the cover of darkness, came Grendel; he carried the wrath of God. He, the evil-doer, intended to ensnare some of the human beings in that high hall. Enraged beneath the heavens, he knew very well the paved road that led to the hall where men were given gifts of gold and drinks of wine. Indeed, that was not the first time that he had sought out the home of Hrothgar; however, never in earlier days (either before or since) would he find stronger heroes among the servants in the hall.

Activity 8.2

Work with a partner or in a small group.

Take it in turns to read the original text out loud.

You will also notice that there are some letters in the original version that are no longer part of the English alphabet. These are:
- æ – known as 'ash' and pronounced *air*
- þ – known as 'thorn' and pronounced as the *th* sound in 'thin'
- Ð/ð – known as 'eth' and pronounced as the *th* sound in 'this'.

Rehearse and practise your performance, ready to perform to the class.

Key skills

Understanding dialect

The influence of Old French

In 1066, Britain was conquered again, this time by Normans from France. The Normans set up a legal and governmental system and their version of French – Old French – became the official language, especially in the south of England.

Over time, Old French and Old English combined and developed into what is now known as **Middle English**.

During this period, there was no one standard form of English being spoken, with variations across the country. The extracts from *Sir Gawain and the Green Knight* and Chaucer on pages 137 and 140–41 will show you an example of the differences between Old French and Old English during this period.

Activity 8.3

There are many **dialects** of modern English, from all over the world.

With a partner, research some of the dialects from these families:
- Caribbean English
- Australian English
- Indian English
- American English

Research the differences between spelling, vocabulary and pronunciation.

Create a short report to present to your class.

I researched different vocabulary for common items such as vehicles, rooms of the house, plants and animals.

I found out common phrases used in different dialects. 'You little ripper!' is from Australia. What do you think it means?

I listened to the different recordings of Caribbean English from different islands. Did you know there are so many different pronouns?

Reading and listening

Middle English poetry

The following extract is from the **anonymous** fourteenth-century poem *Sir Gawain and the Green Knight*. This is a long **narrative poem**, set in the court of the legendary King Arthur, and tells of the strange challenge made by a knight, all green in colour and clothing, to Arthur's court, which is taken up by Arthur's nephew, Sir Gawain.

The symbol 3 represents the letter known as 'yogh', which is no longer in the modern English alphabet. It is pronounced like *ch* in the German word *nicht* and is now indicated by the letters 'gh', as in 'knight' (which in Middle English would have been pronounced *kernicht*).

Spotlight on: Old and Middle English

Old and Middle English can seem very difficult to understand.

Treat this as a code-cracking or problem-solving activity.

Look for clues and hints: make guesses and enjoy uncovering the thoughts of a writer from over 1,000 years ago. These words connect you – isn't that incredible?

HINT

Listen to a reading and try to follow along. You might recognise some of the sounds the more you listen. Search online using the key words 'reading aloud Sir Gawain and the Green Knight' or download an audiobook version with permission.

Extract: *Sir Gawain and the Green Knight*

Þe grene knyʒt vpon grounde grayþely hym dresses,
A littel lut with þe hede, þe lere he discouerez,
His longe louelych lokkez he layd ouer his croun,
Let þe naked nec to þe note schewe.
Gauan gripped to his ax, and gederes hit on hyʒt,
Þe kay fot on þe folde he before sette,
Let him doun lyʒtly lyʒt on þe naked,
Þat þe scharp of þe schalk schyndered þe bones,
And schrank þurʒ þe schyire grece, and schade hit in twynne,
Þat þe bit of þe broun stel bot on þe grounde.
Þe fayre hede fro þe halce hit to þe erþe,
Þat fele hit foyned wyth her fete, þere hit forth roled;
Þe blod brayd fro þe body, þat blykked on þe grene;
And nawþer faltered ne fel þe freke neuer þe helder,
Bot styþly he start forth vpon styf schonkes,
And runyschly he raʒt out, þere as renkkez stoden,
Laʒt to his lufly hed, and lyft hit vp sone;
And syþen boʒez to his blonk, þe brydel he cachchez,
Steppez into stelbawe and strydez alofte,
And his hede by þe here in his honde haldez;
And as sadly þe segge hym in his sadel sette
As non vnhap had hym ayled, þaʒ hedlez he were in stedde.
He brayde his bulk aboute,
Þat vgly bodi þat bledde;
Moni on of hym had doute,
Bi þat his resounz were redde.

Activity 8.4

Try reading the poem on page 137 out loud. Work with a partner – take it in turns to say a line each.

Don't worry if you don't understand everything you read – this is a very distant relation of the English we speak today.

But, as you listen you might notice that you recognise some words, and can guess others.

Make a list of the words you recognise, the words you guess, and the words that sound mysterious, in a table like this:

Words I recognise	Words I can guess	Mysterious sounding words

Translation

Activity 8.5

These are fragments of a translation of *Sir Gawain and the Green Knight* into modern English, but they are muddled up.

It is a gruesome scene, but this is a magical tale – the giant turns out not to be harmed at all!

a Gawain grasped his axe and raised it on high;

b He laid his lovely long locks of hair over the crown of his head allowing his bare neck to be exposed.

c The Green Knight elegantly prepared himself;

d so that the sharp blade shattered through the bones and sheared through the smooth flesh, cutting it in two

e Blood sprayed from the body and flecked on to the green.

f with his head somewhat inclined he revealed his neck.

g so that the bloodied edge of the blade bit into the ground.

h The handsome head fell from the shoulders on to the earth and people kicked out at it with their feet as it rolled towards them.

i he set his left foot on the ground before him and let fall the axe swiftly and cleanly on the naked neck

1 Arrange the fragments into the correct order. Use clues from the ordering of events, and from the original text to help you.
Write the translation in the correct order.

2 The translation is only the beginning of the extract.
Can you find the place where it finishes in the original poem?

3 Create a translation dictionary. Use both texts to create a list of Middle English words matched to modern English words.

Reading and writing

Alliterative poetry

Much modern English poetry uses rhyme as a poetic technique to link words and sounds and highlight the musical aspect of language.

In Old English poetry, alliteration is used instead. This technique uses repeated sounds to bind each line together, forming a kind of language-music.

EXTENSION

Write your own alliterative poem. Choose any subject – your journey to school, an argument with a friend, an imaginary adventure …
Write your poem to include three alliterative words in each line. Do not use rhyme – the alliteration will turn your words into the music of poetry. Have fun with your word choices!

A broken-down bus, battling through traffic
The driver dreams of drifting in a boat on calm water
Laughter leaks from the back, leaving the joke secret.

EXERCISE 8.5

1   Look at the *Beowulf* extract again.

Ða com of more	under misthleoþum
Grendel gongan,	godes yrre bær;
mynte se manscaða	manna cynnes
sumne besyrwan	in sele þam hean.
Wod under wolcnum	to þæs þe he winreced,
goldsele gumena,	gearwost wisse,
fættum fahne.	Ne wæs þæt forma sið
þæt he Hroþgares	ham gesohte;
næfre he on aldordagum	ær ne siþðan
heardran hæle,	healðegnas fand.

Each line is split into two halves – the first half contains one or two repeats, and there is one more repeat in the second half. So, in total, each line has three alliterations.

List three alliterations from each line:

Line 1 – com, more, misthleoþum

Line 2 – …

2   Now look at this further extract from *Sir Gawain*:

> For þe hede in his honde he haldez vp euen,
> Toward þe derrest on þe dece he dressez þe face,
> And hit lyfte vp þe y3e-lyddez and loked ful brode,
> And meled þus much with his muthe, as 3e may now here:
> 'Loke, Gawan, þou be grayþe to go as þou hettez,
> And layte as lelly til þou me, lude, fynde,
> As þou hatz hette in þis halle, herande þise kny3tes;
> To þe grene chapel þou chose, I charge þe, to fotte
> Such a dunt as þou hatz dalt – disserued þou habbez
> To be 3ederly 3olden on Nw 3eres morn.
> Þe kny3t of þe grene chapel men knowen me mony;
> Forþi me for to fynde if þou fraystez, faylez þou neuer.'

Find examples of alliteration in this text.
Are there any rules for how many alliterations appear in each line?

Reading

<u>Author: Geoffrey Chaucer</u>

Geoffrey Chaucer (c.1340-1400) was born in London and is widely celebrated as the most famous poet of the Middle Ages. During his career he was elected a Member of Parliament and was later employed by both King Edward III and King Richard II of England. He was the first poet to be buried in Poets' Corner in Westminster Abbey, in London, where many other famous English poets and playwrights have since been buried.

Chaucer and rhyming couplets

The final extract in this chapter is taken from one of the first major poems to be written in English: *The Canterbury Tales* by Geoffrey Chaucer.

The Canterbury Tales contains a collection of tales in verse supposedly narrated by different members of a group of travellers making their way to the shrine of St Thomas à Becket in Canterbury, to pay their respects. St Thomas à Becket was Archbishop of Canterbury (the senior leader of the Church of England) from 1162 until he was killed in 1170. This type of journey is known as a pilgrimage.

Chaucer's language is much closer to modern English than that of the author of *Sir Gawain and the Green Knight,* who lived at about the same time but in a different part of the country where a different dialect was spoken.

This extract from the Prologue (the introduction of a work) describes the Miller, one of the more grotesque and vulgar members of the pilgrimage. No translation is provided, but the words printed in italics are explained to the right of the poem.

Extract: 'The Miller'

The Miller was a stout *carle* for the nones,	fellow
Full big he was of brawn, and eke of bones;	
That proved well, for *ov'r all where* he came,	wherever
At wrestling he would *bear alway the ram*	win the prize
He was short-shouldered, broad, a *thickegnarr,*	tough, thickset man
There was no door, that he *n'old* heave off bar,	could not
Or break it at a running with his head.	

His beard as any sow or fox was red,

And thereto broad, as though it were a spade.

Upon the *cop* right of his nose he had   tip

A wart, and thereon stood a tuft of hairs

Red as the bristles of a sowe's ears.

His *nose-thirles* blacke were and wide.   nostrils

A sword and buckler bare he by his side.

His mouth as wide was as a furnace.

He was a *jangler*, and a *goliardais*,   joker, buffoon

And that was most of sin and *harlotries*.   crude jokes

Well could he steale corn, and *tolle* thrice   charge

And yet he had a thumb of gold, *pardie*.   good lord

A white coat and a blue hood weared he

A baggepipe well could he blow and soun',

And therewithal he brought us out of town.

Geoffrey Chaucer

The Prologue to the tales is a very important text in the history of England and the English language. It consists of descriptions of the appearance and characters of the pilgrims and allows Chaucer to reveal their particular virtues and vices, providing us with a vivid picture of the people of the fourteenth century and the lives they led, and allowing us to appreciate how little human nature has changed over the centuries.

LET'S TALK

Read the description of the Miller as a class. You will find some parts difficult to understand – but there will be some phrases and descriptions that come to life.

Begin with the parts you do understand, and work together to uncover the parts that you do not fully grasp.

Use these prompts to dig deeper:

■ What sort of person is the Miller?

■ How does the poet use description to tell us the personality of the Miller?

■ Do you know anyone who behaves like the Miller?

Writing

Rhyming couplets

Activity 8.6

Read the poem aloud to a partner or a small group.

Read two lines each. Listen out for the **rhyming couplets** – these are sometimes called Chaucerian couplets.

EXERCISE 8.6

The helpful words printed to the right of the text help with some of the words. However, help is not provided for every single word.

Make a list of the words you do not know. Predict the possible meaning of each word, before checking with your teacher.

Activity 8.7

You are going to write a modern English translation of the following lines:

At wrestling he would *bear alway the ram*	win the prize
He was short-shouldered, broad, a *thickegnarr*,	tough, thickset man
There was no door, that he *n'old* heave off bar,	could not
Or break it at a running with his head.	

1 Read these lines carefully.
2 Work with a partner to discuss the meaning of each line.
3 Re-tell the scene to each other, without looking at the text. Use your memory and the images the words have formed.
4 Discuss the author's intentions. What is the effect he hopes for from these lines?
5 Write a modern version in plain English. It should sound as if you are describing someone to your friends.

EXERCISE 8.7

Write a new version of your alliterative poem using rhyming couplets.

You may find that the rhyming challenge is more difficult than the alliteration!

Reading

Technology and language change

In the second half of the fifteenth century, William Caxton invented the printing press. This invention meant that books, instead of being written by hand, could be produced in large numbers and read by a larger number of people. The result was that a more standardised version of English (that spoken in the south-east) became common throughout England.

LET'S TALK

It might seem old fashioned to us now, but William Caxton's printing press was a very important technological advance that changed the modern world.

His printing press meant that for the first time information could easily be printed and distributed for many people to read.

In the twenty-first century, there is a similar revolution in information technology: the internet.

> The internet is destroying language. Young people only use text-speak and little pictures to communicate.

> The internet shows the power of language. It gives everyone an opportunity to publish their words and ideas. Language has never been more free.

EXERCISE 8.8

Write a persuasive speech in support of one of the opinions expressed in the Let's Talk box.

Include:
- examples of the kinds of language used on the internet – in social media, for example
- a strong introduction that clearly states your position
- well-structured paragraphs to organise and sequence your arguments.

Shakespeare and modern English

By the time of Queen Elizabeth I (1533–1603) and William Shakespeare, the English spoken in the British Isles was similar to the English we speak today and so the period of modern English had begun. The form of English that had developed was a very flexible language; modern English not only contained a very wide vocabulary (drawn from all the different languages that had formed it) but was also able to incorporate words and usage from other languages throughout the world.

Shakespeare was a very inventive writer. He coined over 1,000 new words! To 'coin' a word means to use it for the first time.

Although Shakespeare's language can be difficult for modern listeners to understand, it is in fact modern English – with most of the words and rules we use today.

Author: William Shakespeare

William Shakespeare (1564-1616) was an English playwright, poet and actor. He is regarded as one of the greatest writers in the English language and the world's greatest dramatist.

Activity 8.8

With a partner, investigate the meanings of these words and phrases, first coined by Shakespeare:

We are such stuff as dreams are made on

Oh I am fortune's fool!

The King's name is a tower of strength

Better a witty fool than a foolish wit.

Though I am not naturally honest, I am so sometimes by chance

The game's afoot

Uneasy lies the head that wears a crown.

Writing and key skills

> **HINT**
> Remember that the technical term for the study of the origins of words is etymology.

Word origins

The English language continued to evolve during the eighteenth and nineteenth centuries, particularly as trade and political agreements were established around the world. Words from other countries became part of English, such as 'sherbet' from the Middle East and 'moccasin' from North America.

EXERCISE 8.9

Here is an opportunity for you to undertake some etymological research into the origins of some English vocabulary. Here are six lists of words. Each list contains words that have entered the English language from different sources or roots: Celtic, French, Greek, Latin, Old English, Old Norse or other sources.

Draw up a table like the one on the next page. Using a dictionary or online search tool, investigate the origins and meanings of the words in the lists and write them in your table under the correct heading. (Some words have been filled in already to start you off.)

1   apple, berserk, bonanza, costume, delta, glen, manuscript, syrup, tambourine
2   academy, algebra, brogue, equestrian, fog, guitar, mustard, potato, sword
3   billiards, bungalow, cairn, civilian, fork, jungle, midnight, mohair, skirt, theory
4   albatross, anchor, coffee, daughter, elegance, khaki, punctuation, saga, slogan

5 animal, bacteria, brother, canoe, crag, foyer, guest, pyjama, shampoo

6 alliance, armada, banshee, encyclopedia, ghost, mosquito, nocturnal, outlaw, thug

	Celtic	French	Greek	Latin	Old English	Old Norse	Other sources
1			delta				
2	brogue						
3				civilian			jungle
4							
5							
6							

HINT

This is quite a complicated activity and, depending on the time available, you may need either to reduce its scope or to plan to engage in it over several weeks as an ongoing piece of research. Remember that watching television programmes and films made in other parts of the world may be a convenient way of collecting examples of the use of English in those countries.

KEY WORDS

slang informal, conversational words or phrases, often peculiar to a particular age group; for example, It was a *really cool* gig

colloquial describing informal language used in everyday conversations

Key skills

Slang and informal language

LET'S TALK

This activity is intended to explore how the form of English that you speak when you are with people of your own age and circumstances differs from both Standard English and the English spoken by people of an older generation. It will involve careful organisation.

■ Work in a medium-sized group – ideally between eight and ten people with a balance of male and female contributors. If possible, members of the group should be from different cultural backgrounds, or have joined your school after living in another country.

■ The first stage of this activity involves collecting a list of the most common **slang** or **colloquial** terms that you use and the names that you apply to everyday objects and activities. Do all members of the group use the same expressions or does the vocabulary differ? Discuss why this might be the case; for example, do the terms differ from those used in other countries or different parts of your own country? Are there any other similarities or differences between groups that you notice? You might also consider differences in grammatical usage. Once you have assembled a list of these expressions, discuss among yourselves whether you think that they are Standard English expressions and, if not, what you think the Standard English equivalents are.

■ The next stage (to be carried out on a different day and working in a pair) is to interview a willing adult who is at least a generation or so older than you and to ask them about the expressions you have identified. Do they understand the expressions to mean the same as you do? If they don't, then ask them what words they would use and keep a note of this.

■ Finally, reassemble with your original group and pool the results of your interviews. What has the experience taught you about the need to use a form of the English language that can be understood by all users, regardless of age and circumstances? Perhaps you could even combine and write a dictionary of teenage usage aimed at people in older generations.

Reviewing

Reflect on your learning in this chapter.

Reading

■ The language in Chaucer's *The Canterbury Tales* is written in Old English. Did you find it interesting? Did you find it challenging?

Speaking and listening

■ Did you contribute to the discussion about English and other languages? Did you learn anything new from the other contributors?
■ How did you feel about speaking, and listening to others speaking, in another dialect? Did you find it challenging in any way?

Writing

■ Did you enjoy writing your alliterative poem? Why or why not?

Key skills

■ List up to five new words you have learned.
■ What new key skills have you learned since the start of the year?

Further reading

If you enjoyed reading these extracts, you might enjoy:
■ *Introduction to Old English* (third edition) by Peter Baker
■ *Beowulf* by Michael Morpurgo
There are websites online that provide 'translations' of Chaucer's *The Canterbury Tales* for younger learners.
If you are interested in the history of this time, you could try *Invasion, Plague and Murder* by Aaron Wilkes.

9 What a performance!

Reading
- ★ An extract from a modern play (cultural context)
- ★ An extract from a Shakespeare play, focusing on historical context
- ★ An extract from a novel

Speaking and listening
- ★ Listening to praise poems
- ★ Listening to a story about performance
- ★ Acting a scene from a play
- ★ Exploring non-verbal communication

WHAT A PERFORMANCE!

Writing
- ★ Writing a praise poem
- ★ Writing a scene from a play
- ★ Writing a one-act play in groups

Key skills
- ★ Non-verbal communication

LET'S TALK
- ■ Do you prefer to watch or listen to drama, or do you prefer to read it? Why?
- ■ What other techniques do actors use aside from speaking their lines?
- ■ What clues do you get from these techniques? How do they help your understanding of a story?

Speaking and listening

Praise poems

Praise poems are created to praise achievements and people – leaders or ordinary people. They can also serve as reminders to people about what is expected of them. In some cultures, it is common for people to write praise poems about themselves. They can also praise animals!

Praise poems are meant to be performed. The language used in them is chosen carefully in order to attract the attention of listeners. Imagery such as similes and metaphors are often used.

Activity 9.1

1   Listen to the praise poems on the audio. The first one is a poem that praises a woman farmer for her physical and emotional strength in providing for her family, caring for her herd of goats and working the land.

> ### The Farmer
> Early every morning you begin your toil
> Feeding the animals and tilling the soil
> In hot weather and in cold
> Your growing herd of goats provide milk
> Which you turn into butter and cheese
> As hardworking as a little bee
> But as strong as a buffalo
> You are a hero in your village
> Fearless, caring, a mother to all
> And a fine farmer too…

2 Then listen to this modern praise poem, written by a student in praise of herself.

> I am a daughter of this land
> A sister to you all.
> From across the sea my family came
> For a new beginning, a change.
> An immigrant I am and proud to be
> Enriched by a new culture, not forgetting my own.
> Now I am a bird
> Flying high
> With wings that can take me anywhere.
> I am someone with the courage to fly
> Someone who wants to fly.

3 Work in a group. Discuss what each poem is about.
- What imagery is used and what does this add to the meaning?
- Describe the form of each poem.

Activity 9.2

1 Choose one of the praise poems above and explain why you are drawn to it over the other. In your group, discuss how you could perform it:
- What is the aim of the poem?
- Who is the audience going to be?
- What parts of the poem would you emphasise?
- How would you use body language to give depth to the meaning?

2 Perform your poem in your group.

3 Discuss the different ways in which the poems were performed.
- Which performance was the most effective? Why?
- Did all the performances convey the same meaning?

Don't be afraid to ask for feedback.

HINT

Try to be spontaneous. If the words don't sound right, change them until you find the words that work. You can change a praise poem each time you perform it and become more confident.

EXERCISE 9.1

Make up a praise poem about yourself or, if you feel uncomfortable doing that, compose a poem about someone else whom you admire, or an animal. Try to do this orally. Make notes of words and phrases that you want to use. Adapt your language to suit your purpose and get across your ideas clearly.

Listening and writing

In the spotlight

You are going to listen to a short story which describes how someone felt before and during a performance. The story was written by a learner in high school. The story is a little like a **monologue** in a play, in which a character lets us know what is going through his or her head at a given moment.

Activity 9.3

Have you had to give a performance of any kind recently? How do you feel before and during a performance?

Work in a group and brainstorm some words and phrases that describe how you felt. Think about all of your senses. You could use a diagram like this:

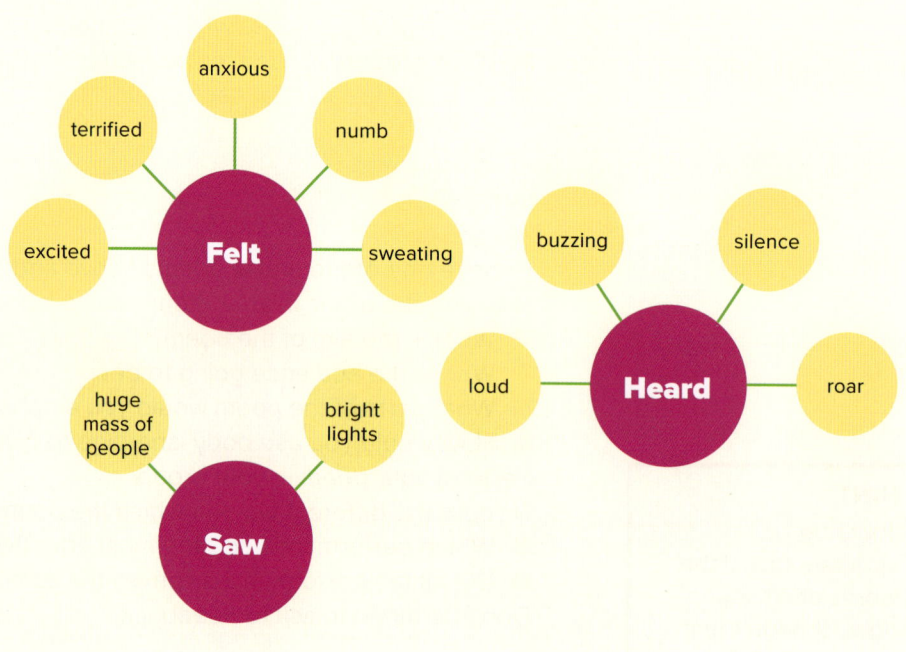

Activity 9.4

Listen to the audio again and tell a partner what it is all about.
For example:
1 What performance did the writer give?
2 How did he feel about it at the beginning of the story?
3 How did he feel at the end? What changed?

EXERCISE 9.2

Read this paragraph from the text you have heard. Comment on the writer's use of sentences to create an effect. What types of sentences does he use (simple, complex or compound – see page 16)? Why?

> My fingers clamp down on the strings. Three seconds. Are my fingers in the right place? Two seconds. I'm cold. One second. My heart throbs as it pumps blood through my veins. I breathe in. Cue. My right hand starts picking at the strings while my left hand dances around the frets. Moments later I start singing into the microphone, my voice cracking under the strain of the cold before it reaches its full strength.

EXERCISE 9.3

Read the following sentences and identify one spelling mistake in each sentence.

Correct the mistake and then discuss with a partner what you need to remember about each word. Is there a spelling rule that you can apply?

1 The smell of the hot, sweeting fans begins to fade from my nostrils.
2 The intermitent thumps of my fingers sliding over the frets are in unison with my heartbeat.
3 My fingers run up and down the neck of my gitar.
4 I inhale sharply, cold air filing my nostrils.
5 The increasing roar of the chearing crowd becomes more distant in my mind.
6 Electrisity pulsing through me.

EXERCISE 9.4

Write a paragraph describing how you have felt or think you would feel before and during a performance. Use different types of sentences (simple, complex and compound) to create the effect that you want (such as anxiety, relaxation, etc.).

HINT

Describe what your senses feel, hear, see and smell.

Use repetition, sentence length and word choice to enhance the meaning. Try to include a metaphor or simile if you can.

Reading

A modern play

> **Activity 9.5**
>
> Before you read both extracts from *The Return* below aloud, look at it quickly and, with a partner, discuss and answer these questions:
>
> 1 Which of the characters appear in this **scene**?
> 2 What do you know about the setting (time and place)? Read the **stage directions** quickly.
> 3 What do these words refer to in the setting description: Stage Right, Downstage Left, Downstairs Right?
>
> Read and discuss the words in the glossary box.

Author: Fatima Dike

Fatima Dike is an award-winning South African playwright and theatre maker. She was born in Langa in Cape Town in South Africa and wrote her first play *The Sacrifice of Kreli* in 1976, in English and isiXhosa, which is a language spoken by many people in South Africa. The extract that you will read is from a play called *The Return*.

KEY WORDS

acts and **scenes** the sections that plays are divided into (like chapters in novels). A change of setting or time is usually indicated by a new scene.

character lists give additional information about the characters in a play, and sometimes about what they look like, what age they are and how they are dressed

stage directions notes to help the actors, often put in brackets or in italics. Actors do not say the stage instructions.

GLOSSARY

kraal – a place where animals are kept

Gugulethu – a suburb next to Langa

Read the first extract, which includes the **character list** and the settings. The second extract, on the next page, is from **Act** 1 Scene 2.

Extract: *The Return* (1)

Characters

Zwelibanzi Somdaka, also known as Tata, 60

Nozizwe Somdaka, also known as Mama, 56

Buntu Somdaka, Son, 38

Isis Somdaka, Daughter-in-law, 34

Sisi

Sangoma

Settings

Kitchen of a house in Langa. A stove, a fridge, a microwave, a dresser, a kitchen table, four chairs, a TV set, easy chairs in front of the TV.

Stage Right, a bedroom. A dressing table, two easy chairs – this will be referred to as the Buntu/Isis Bedroom.

Downstage Left, the garden of the house. A set of steps leads down to the garden from the kitchen. A bench in the garden.

Downstairs Right, the **kraal**; graveyards at **Gugulethu** and at Langa.

Time – 2008

Spotlight on: cultural context

When we read any work of imaginative literature we first of all approach it with the beliefs and values of our own society. There are some values (such as showing respect to older people or respecting other people's lives and property) that are common to all societies. However, we should not assume that the world in which the characters exist is exactly the same as the world we live in.

Activity 9.6

Work in a group of five.

1 Decide who will read each character role.
2 Read the extract aloud in your group.
3 Answer the following questions in your group to make sure you understand the extract.
   a Who is Sisi and what is her role in this home?

b How does the writer use punctuation to show us what the characters are feeling?
c How would you describe the characters of Mama and Tata in this extract?
d How do you think Isis feels?

4 Read the play aloud again and improve your performance, based on your discussions.

HINT

The first time you read this extract, you will need to read ahead so that you can read your role in a way that makes sense.

Think about the age of your character and the tone of voice the character would use.

Look at the punctuation. How can you use this to add to the meaning and the drama of the situation?

Extract: *The Return* (2)

Scene 2

Day 2, Wednesday. Three months later, early in the morning. Kitchen and the BUNTU/ISIS bedroom.

TATA is watching the traffic report on TV. MAMA is frying egg, bacon, slicing tomatoes and frying them too. She will keep them warm in the warmer drawer. The kettle boils and MAMA makes coffee.

…

Mama I wonder why Buntu wouldn't allow us to fetch him from the airport? (*Just then a car stops outside, doors open and close. MAMA runs upstage, looks off right. Coming back and calling out into the garden.*) Sisi! Sisi … come, quickly … (*SISI enters from the garden and runs into the kitchen.*) Quickly, hurry, Sisi … they are here! (*SISI exits.*) Ngabo, it's them!

In her excitement, MAMA tries to run out to meet them. TATA restrains her. Eventually BUNTU enters, followed by ISIS, the picture of New York fashion. They each carry a suitcase. SISI comes in with two extra bags. She sets them down.

Buntu Mama! Tata!

BUNTU puts down his suitcase and hugs his father.

Tata Buntu! (*He puts his hands on BUNTU's shoulders as if to measure how wide they are. He takes his hand and shakes it but also looking at the size of it. They hug again.*) Welcome, my son.

GLOSSARY

sommer – Afrikaans word which means 'just'

ewe – isiXhosa word which means 'yes'

Mama runs her hands over Buntu's face, looks at the fingers of each hand carefully, then she puts her hands around his face and kisses him on both cheeks. MAMA turns to ISIS, looks at her, taking in her slender, model figure. ISIS slips her suitcase on to the floor. Then MAMA embraces her. ISIS turns to move over to TATA. MAMA intercepts her and she brings ISIS over to TATA. He embraces her.

Welcome home, my daughter. Buntu, Isis, this is Sisi – she helps us twice a week.

Buntu/Isis/Sisi Hi! Again.

Mama Er … Sisi, take the suitcases to their bedroom … come along, now. We've got a lovely bedroom suite for you, sitting room and all …

SISI does so. The Africans sit down, wiping tears from their eyes. ISIS stays standing, waiting for an invitation to sit. SISI comes from the bedroom and stands in the shadows towards the back.

Tata Excuse me, Isis, have you come into my house to fight with us?

Isis *(confused)* I … fight … no, no, of course …

There is some gentle laughter from the others.

Tata My child, if someone comes into our house and stands, it means that the person is not coming in peace.

Buntu In America, we wait until we're asked to sit. Sweetheart, here you just **sommer** sit!

ISIS does so.

Mama *(in isiXhosa)* **Ewe**, Buntu, your accent hasn't changed much, I can still understand you. My child, we must praise God and your ancestors for bringing you home back whole. So many years! I didn't think I'd see you in this life again. No, we must give thanks to God for bringing you back in one piece.

TATA rises and turns off the TV.

Activity 9.7

In your group, write a scene for a new play. Imagine someone in your family went away and came back after a long time. How would the family react? What would they do and say?

Your scene should:
- be about the same length as the extract you have just read
- have between three and five characters
- include a character list
- include stage directions.

HINT

You can try to improvise the scene first (in theatre, this is called 'ad-libbing'). Discuss your characters and assume your roles. Then speak and act spontaneously and see what happens. Stop and discuss the scene, then write it down with stage directions and polish it.

DID YOU KNOW?

An anachronism is the name given to an error when an author includes something from the wrong period of time; for example, having sixteenth-century characters using mobile phones.

Even the greatest authors are sometimes guilty of this. William Shakespeare in his play *Julius Caesar*, which is set in ancient Rome, describes a clock striking. Striking clocks were not invented until at least a thousand years after the events described in his play.

Activity 9.8

Read this extract from *Romeo and Juliet* with your teacher. You can also listen to the audio.

In this extract from the play, 14-year-old Juliet has secretly married Romeo, who has been sent away for killing her cousin Tybalt in a swordfight. Unaware that their daughter is married, her parents, Lord and Lady Capulet, have arranged a marriage for Juliet to the rich Count Paris. In this scene (which has been slightly edited) Juliet is informed that the arranged marriage will take place very soon.

Spotlight on: historical context

The historical context of fiction that is set in the sixteenth century will be very different from the context in which modern readers live. It will reflect some social and historical attitudes of the time in which it was written. For example, we do not expect the characters to use mobile phones! The author creates the world of the past for the reader through describing the setting (time and place) and the actions and words of the character. We need to take this into account when we read or write historical fiction.

Extract: *Romeo and Juliet*

Lady Capulet: Well, well, thou hast a careful father, child;
　　　　　　One who, to put thee from thy heaviness,
　　　　　　Hath sorted out a sudden day of joy,
　　　　　　That thou expect'st not nor I look'd not for.

Juliet: Madam, in happy time, what day is that?

Lady Capulet: Marry, my child, early next Thursday morn,
　　　　　　The gallant, young and noble gentleman,
　　　　　　The County Paris, at Saint Peter's Church,
　　　　　　Shall happily make thee there a joyful bride.

Juliet: Now, by Saint Peter's Church and Peter too,
　　　He shall not make me there a joyful bride
　　　I wonder at this haste; that I must wed
　　　Ere he, that should be husband, comes to woo.
　　　I pray you, tell my lord and father, madam,
　　　I will not marry yet; and, when I do, I swear,
　　　It shall be Romeo, whom you know I hate,
　　　Rather than Paris. These are news indeed!

Lady Capulet: Here comes your father; tell him so yourself,
　　　　　　And see how he will take it at your hands.
　　　　　　Enter Capulet and Nurse.

Capulet: When the sun sets, the air doth drizzle dew;
But for the sunset of my brother's son
It rains downright.
How now! a **conduit**, girl? what, still in tears?
Evermore showering? In one little body
Thou counterfeit'st a bark, a sea, a wind;
For still thy eyes, which I may call the sea,
Do ebb and flow with tears; the bark thy body is,
Sailing in this salt flood; the winds, thy sighs;
Who, raging with thy tears, and they with them,
Without a sudden calm, will overset
Thy tempest-tossed body How now, wife!
Have you deliver'd to her our decree?

Lady Capulet: Ay, sir; but she will none, she gives you thanks.
I would the fool were married to her grave!

Capulet: Soft! take me with you, take me with you, wife.
How! will she none? doth she not give us thanks?
Is she not proud? doth she not count her blest,
Unworthy as she is, that we have wrought
So worthy a gentleman to be her bridegroom?

Juliet: Good father, I beseech you on my knees,
Hear me with patience but to speak a word.

Capulet: Hang thee, young baggage! disobedient wretch!
I tell thee what: get thee to church o' Thursday,
Or never after look me in the face:
Speak not, reply not, do not answer me;
My fingers itch.

Lady Capulet: You are too hot.

Capulet: God's bread! it makes me mad:
Day, night, hour, tide, time, work, play,
Alone, in company, still my care hath been
To have her **match'd**: and having now provided
A gentleman of noble parentage,
Of fair **demesnes**, youthful, and nobly train'd,
Stuff'd, as they say, with honourable parts,
Proportion'd as one's thought would wish a man;
And then to have a wretched **puling** fool,
A whining **mammet**, in her fortune's tender,
To answer 'I'll not wed; I cannot love,
I am too young; I pray you, pardon me.'
But, as you will not wed, I'll pardon you:
Graze where you will you shall not house with me:
Look to't, think on't, I do not use to jest.

GLOSSARY

conduit – a pipe or passage to carry water

match'd – married

demesnes – property

puling – whimpering

mammet – doll

forsworn – break my word

Thursday is near; lay hand on heart, advise:
An you be mine, I'll give you to my friend;
An you be not, hang, beg, starve, die in the streets,
For, by my soul, I'll ne'er acknowledge thee,
Nor what is mine shall never do thee good:
Trust to't, bethink you; I'll not be **forsworn**.
Exit.

Juliet: Is there no pity sitting in the clouds,
That sees into the bottom of my grief?
O, sweet my mother, cast me not away!
Delay this marriage for a month, a week;
Or, if you do not, make the bridal bed
In that dim monument where Tybalt lies.

Lady Capulet: Talk not to me, for I'll not speak a word:
Do as thou wilt, for I have done with thee.

Activity 9.9

In Shakespeare's time, children, especially girls, were expected to obey their parents without question. What do you learn from the extract about the attitude of Juliet's parents towards their daughter and of Juliet's behaviour towards them? Work in a group to answer the following questions and discuss the historical context of this extract.

1 What does Lord Capulet say and do? Look at the language he uses. For example, what is suggested by his use of words like 'whining mammet' and 'Graze where you will'? Which other words can you identify that demonstrate how he feels?

2 What does Lady Capulet say and do? Look at the way she responds to Juliet at the end of the scene.

3 What does Juliet say and do? Think about the situation she is in at the start of the scene and how she behaves towards both her parents.

EXERCISE 9.5
Write a paragraph about this extract. Explain briefly what it is about and how the actions of the characters reflect the historical context. Give examples.

Activity 9.10

Work in a small group and practise reading this extract aloud. Think about how you would use your voice to portray the characters.

EXTENSION
Watch one of the film versions of *Romeo and Juliet*. There are many to choose from.

Retell or summarise the story orally. Then discuss these questions:
■ Which actors do you think portrayed the historical context well?
■ Why do you think this story is still popular so many years after it was written?

Author: Ruth Prawer Jhabvala

Ruth Prawer Jhabvala (1927–2013) was a novelist and screenwriter. She was born in Germany but lived in England, India and New York. She is well known for her novels, stories and for her work in the film industry.

EXERCISE 9.6

By yourself, read carefully this extract from 'The Young Couple' by Ruth Prawer Jhabvala.

WORD ATTACK SKILLS

Explain the meaning of the following words and phrases as they are used in the extract:

✔ involuntarily
✔ confided
✔ complex
✔ taunts
✔ obtrusive
✔ customarily
✔ tart

Extract: 'The Young Couple'

Cathy, an English woman, has married Naraian, an Indian, and returned to India to live with him and his family. She finds it difficult to adjust to the culture of her husband's country and in this extract from the story we see how she unintentionally behaves in an unacceptable way.

Of course, it was not easy to do anything decisive and independent while they were living the way they were, with Naraian's family supporting them completely; and the most important step now was for Naraian to get himself a job to support the two of them. But, as they both fully agreed, it was no use rushing anything; he had to have time to look around and weigh possibilities, so that in the end he would have something beautiful and useful where he would be fully engaged. In the meanwhile, Cathy would have been glad to help out and get a job herself. She had done quite a lot of things in England, she had been a receptionist to a Harley Street specialist, a sales assistant in an airlines office. Once for a brief while a waitress in a coffee bar, but of course she realised that it was impossible to do anything like that here because of her, or rather the family's, background and social standing. The sort of jobs this background and social standing permitted her she was not qualified to do.

Nevertheless, often nowadays, after Naraian had gone out, she lay on the bed, on her stomach, one foot with a silver slipper dangling from it up in the air, her fingers twisting and untwisting the end of her golden plait, and read the Situations Vacant columns in the newspapers. It was depressing: there was nothing, nothing at all for her. It was all either for readers and senior lecturers in sociology, or for fitters and mill-inspectors preferably with experience in small-grind machines. Soon her eyes **involuntarily** slipped to the matrimonial columns, which amused her. But she felt frustrated.

Also, perhaps, a little bored and lonely. She met plenty of people but they were all Naraian's friends or his family, so that she began to feel almost as if they were forming a ring round her out of which she could not break. She **confided** this impression to Naraian, who scorned it. She was free, he insisted, to do exactly as she liked, go wherever she wanted. But where was she to go, what was there to do? She never liked to go anywhere without Naraian, and there was certainly no question of walking freely down the road: she was stared at, sometimes mocked for being white and different, certainly always an object of attention.

Sometimes, when it seemed to her that she was getting a **complex** about this, she decided to brave the stares and **taunts** and go by herself into the city bazaar. Actually, it wasn't so bad: she drew a lot of attention but she ignored it. She pretended to merge with the crowd of modestly veiled women, sick cows, pickpockets, and **obtrusive** hawkers.

When she got home, she was breathless but quite excited. She spread her purchases on the bed with a feeling of triumph: they were invariably things she didn't need – a red velvet purse sewn over with silver spangles, green and gold sandals, a picture of a swan reflected in a lake which was made out of a piece of mirror – but she was proud and pleased with herself for having gone out to buy them.

One Sunday, at lunch with Naraian's family, she was questioned about these excursions of hers. It seemed she had been seen (one was always seen, there were so many relatives, so many acquaintances, so much time in which to pass the word around) and what had excited particular comment was that she had been alone and on foot. 'Where is the need?' said Naraian's mother.

'One word, and I shall come myself with the car to take you.' This was true: Naraian's mother, sisters, sisters-in-law, always eager to go out shopping in a car, frequently urged her to join them. But she had enjoyed herself more on her own. She looked for help to Naraian, but he was busy eating a mango; either he hadn't heard, or he didn't want to get involved. She would have welcomed a word from him to tell his family about the independence **customarily** enjoyed as a right by English girls. No such word coming, Naraian's mother drove her point home further: 'Our girls don't go into these bazaars alone. It is not proper for us.'

There was a waiting pause. Cathy knew she was now expected to make a **tart** reply which would instigate her mother-in-law to an even tarter one, after which it would be her turn again, and so on until they had got a really good family row going. But Cathy didn't say anything. Unlike the others, she had no liking for these family rows. Instead she looked again towards Naraian, who was now busy eating the flesh round the stone of his mango, always a delicate operation calling for all one's concentration and skill. Cathy lowered her head, lifted the napkin from her lap, and folded it several times very neatly. She sensed disappointment in the air, as if she had let everyone down.

Ruth Prawer Jhabvala

EXERCISE 9.7

This story focuses on the clash between two cultures and their values. By referring closely to the extract, explain fully how the way in which Cathy, Naraian and Naraian's mother behave illustrates the differences between the European society in which Cathy was brought up and the one she has now moved into.

Activity 9.11

Work in a group and dramatise a scene from this story in a spontaneous way, without writing a play script. Think about the characters and what they would say or do.

Spotlight on: tone of voice

Tone of voice is the emotion or mood that characters show in their voice to communicate their feelings and enhance meaning. Register refers to how friendly (informal) or formal the language is that the actors or characters use. Characters or actors can also change the pace of their voice (for example, speaking faster when they are excited and more slowly when they are confused) or volume (for example, speaking louder when they are angry, excited or happy, and more softly when they are sad).

Key Skills

Non-verbal communication

We are able to convey a lot of meaning without saying anything. We can use our bodies as well as props and costumes to communicate in a non-verbal way with others.

Examples of non-verbal communication include:
- facial expressions: smiling, frowning
- body movements: moving our hands around, our posture, walking fast or slowly, touching others
- eye contact: looking at or away from someone we are talking to
- appearance: dressing in a certain way, wearing a costume.

Non-verbal communication can be positive or negative, conscious or unconscious. We can tell a lot about how a person is feeling through their body language. If we feel nervous, for example, this may show in the way we move our hands or the expression on our face.

For actors in plays and films, non-verbal communication is an important part of creating a character.

Speaking and writing

Activity 9.12

1 Work in a group to choose a scene from a play you have read in this chapter or elsewhere. If different groups perform the same scene, you could compare them afterwards.
2 In your group, prepare to perform the scene by thinking about your audience.
   - Who are they? How can you help them understand the play?
   - How can you create an impact on them? For example, some audiences may enjoy humour and exaggerated body language, while others may prefer a more serious approach.
   Think about the cultural and historical context and how you will create a distinctive voice for each character. Consider:
   - make-up and costume
   - the props you will need
   - the language (dialogue) in the script
   - the non-verbal language, such as movement, facial expressions and gestures
   - how the actors should say the lines: the pace (how fast or slow), tone of voice and register (formal or informal).
3 In your group, act the scene for your class.
4 Take some time to reflect on the performances. Discuss the different interpretations and use of non-verbal communication techniques. What had the biggest impact? Why?

Activity 9.13

Work as a group and write a short one-act play with a specific cultural or historical context.

Here are some ideas:
- A cousin who grew up in another country comes to visit your family
- A modern version of *Romeo and Juliet*, or a version set in a different cultural context

You can find many templates online to use as the basis for planning a play. Or you could use a storyboard or mind map.

Follow the steps given on the writing cycle on page viii.

When you write your play, remember to:
- Use the correct writing conventions for play scripts (punctuation, layout, etc.).
- Give each actor a distinctive voice. Think about the words they will use, the gestures or movements they will make, the props they will need and how they will interact with other characters. You can do this by writing notes about the characters at the beginning and by writing stage directions.

HINT

Remember, use each writing task to develop your handwriting. Over time your handwriting should become easier to read and easier to write: keep track of this by comparing your current handwriting with previous writing tasks and note any areas for improvement. Keep your handwriting in a flowing style.

EXTENSION

Write your own script for a movie or TV show. Although you will only be writing a single scene, you need to think about the whole play.
- What type of movie or TV show is it? Who are the audience / viewers? How will they relate to the characters / actors?
- Which movies or TV shows are similar to this? How will yours be different?
- What language will you use to create each character and to give them a distinctive voice?
- What location (setting), props and costumes will you need?
- How can you use more adjectives, adverbs and connectives to make your language more interesting?
- What staging instructions do you need to provide?

Reviewing

Reflect on your learning in this chapter.

Reading

- Which of the texts in this chapter did you most enjoy reading? Why?
- *Romeo and Juliet* is written in Old Elizabethan English. How do you feel about this? Did you find it interesting? Did you find it challenging?
- How did you feel about reading lines aloud and acting in a play? Has your confidence grown during Year 8?

Speaking and listening

- Did you enjoy listening to your classmates read their praise poems aloud? Did you have a favourite? Why was it your favourite?
- Will you consider listening to more spoken word / poetry – perhaps a podcast? Why? Why not?
- During group work, did you feel able to contribute to the discussion? Has your confidence grown during Year 8?

Writing

- Did you write a praise poem about yourself? Or did you find it a challenge? Why? Why not?
- Writing a play is quite different from writing a traditional story. Did you enjoy the task? Did you find any aspect challenging?

Key skills

- List up to five new words you have learned.
- What key skills have you learned since the start of the year?

Further reading

If you enjoyed reading these extracts, you might enjoy:
- *A Raisin in the Sun* by Lorraine Hansberry
- *A Midsummer Night's Dream* by William Shakespeare

Glossary

acts and **scenes** the sections that plays are divided into (like chapters in novels). A change of setting or time is usually indicated by a new scene

adjective a word that is used to describe a noun, e.g. the *red* house

adverb a word, frequently ending in *-ly*, that is used to describe the action expressed by a verb, e.g. Joe ate *hungrily.*

alliteration the repetition of consonant sounds at the beginning of word . This technique is used to link words and lodge phrases into the memory, and is often used in brand names and advertising

anecdote a short recount of an event, usually humorous or interesting

angle the point of view behind a writer's presentation of a topic

anonymous without name, or name unknown. Many old poems and texts are said to be 'anonymous', meaning there is no record of the specific author. It is sometimes shortened to 'anon'

anticlimax/bathos the final element in a list that trivialises the seriousness of the preceding elements

apostrophe a punctuation mark (') indicating possession or omission

assonance the repetition of the same or similar vowel sounds within words, phrases or sentences

atmosphere how the physical situation or environment feels

audience the people for whom authors have written their work

author brief this explains very clearly the purpose and form an author needs to use in a piece of written work. Professional authors are sent briefs as part of their contract. They must make sure they include all of the information and details required

autobiography a true story about someone's life, told by that person

bathos *see* **anticlimax**

bias a particular feeling either for or against something, sometimes resulting from prejudice

caesura a pause in a verse where one phrase ends and another phrase begins. The pause is often shown by a comma

caption a title or explanation for a picture or illustration

character lists give additional information about the characters in a play, and sometimes about what they look like, what age they are and how they are dressed

clause a group of words containing a verb. A *main* clause makes sense on its own; a *subordinate* clause depends on a main clause for its sense to be clear

climax a list, often consisting of three elements, in which each element intensifies the statement made by the previous one

colloquial describing informal language used in everyday conversations

colon (:) introduces something that is to follow

columns the vertical blocks of print into which a page of a newspaper or magazine is divided

complex sentence a long sentence consisting of interlinked main and subordinate clauses and phrases

compound sentence a sentence consisting of two or more main clauses linked by coordinating conjunctions

connective any word that links clauses, sentences or ideas together

culture a particular way of life, including the customs and traditions, beliefs, knowledge and behaviours of a particular group of people at a particular time

dash a punctuation mark used to indicate an interruption to the main structure of a sentence

dialect a variant of a language which may:
- be primarily a spoken form, often with a strong accent
- be shared by a particular group - often from a certain place or region
- use different vocabulary for some words
- have differences in spelling
- have some slight differences in grammar.

A dialect of a language is not a new language. If two people speak different dialects of English, they will be able to understand each other with only very few difficulties.

direct speech the words actually spoken by someone, indicated by speech marks ('…')

emotive language words chosen by writers deliberately to arouse feelings in their readers

enjambment a term used to describe lines of poetry that run on from one line to the next without a pause

epic a long narrative poem which usually tells of the heroic deeds of a person of great courage and bravery

extended metaphor an implied comparison that is continued over several lines or paragraphs in writing

factual information information that is accurate and true. This can be found in texts such as textbooks, encyclopedias, recipes and timetables

fantasy a genre of fiction with unreal settings, often inspired by real-world myth and folklore

first-person narration (using 'I') telling the story from one of the character's point of view

foil someone or something that makes another person's good or bad qualities more noticeable

formal formal writing or speech uses a serious tone and is often used in professional settings and for letters, reports and academic essays. Standard punctuation and grammar are used and contractions are avoided

free verse a poem with no fixed or regular structure

genre a particular type of literature or other art form, e.g. novel, poetry, science fiction

headlines words printed in large letters as the title of a story in a newspaper

homographs words that have the same spelling but different pronunciations and meanings

homonyms words that have the same spelling and pronunciation, but different meanings

homophones words that have the same pronunciation but different spellings and meanings

human interest the aspect of a story in a newspaper that describes the experiences or emotions of individuals to which readers can relate

hyperbole deliberate exaggeration

inflected Old English, or Anglo-Saxon, is an inflected language. In Old English, the endings of nouns change to indicate which case they are (subject, object, possessive, etc.) and the endings of verbs also change depending on whether they are first, second or third person, singular or plural. Many modern languages are inflected, such as German, French and Spanish

informal informal writing or speech takes a more casual, conversational or personal tone and may include slang or figures of speech and non-standard English

irony using words that are the opposite of what you mean, often for comic effect

legend a traditional story, involving humans with extraordinary skills, sometimes based on real historical figures and real events

litotes a deliberate understatement that is made to give emphasis

metaphor an indirect comparison in which it is implied that one thing is another, e.g. The banner of smoke flew from the factory chimney.

meter the regular recurring rhythmic pattern of stressed and unstressed syllables on which a poem is based

Middle English the form of English language spoken and written between the Norman Conquest (1066 CE) and the late fifteenth century

monologue a long speech by one actor in a play or film

mood the emotional setting; the feeling a reader gets when reading a poem

myth a traditional story, especially one concerning the early history of a people or explaining a natural or social phenomenon, and often involving supernatural beings or events

narrative poem a poem that tells a story

noun a word that gives the name of a person, place, thing or abstract idea

novel a work of fiction, usually written in a book

oxymoron a figure of speech that combines two normally contradictory terms to create a special effect

paradox a situation or statement that seems impossible because it contains two contradictory facts

paragraph a group of closely related sentences that develop a central or main idea

passive voice when the subject is acted on by the verb, e.g. *the ball was kicked by the player*. This is the opposite to the active voice: *the player kicked the ball*

persona a role or character taken on by a writer

personality what a person's character and behaviour are like

personification a literary device which presents a thing or an abstract idea as a person

phrase a group of words that do not contain a verb, e.g. She ate her breakfast *while on the bus.*

prefix a letter or group of letters attached to the beginning of a word that partly affects its meaning

present participle a word formed from a verb ending in '-ing', used as an adjective or to form a verb tense

purpose the reason or intention for writing the piece, e.g. to amuse, to inform, to entertain

quest a long and difficult search or an expedition, often by a knight, to accomplish a task

register how friendly (informal) or formal the language is that the characters use

repetition to repeat words or phrases again and again

rhyme when the endings of two or more words sound alike, e.g. *lean* and *seen*

rhyme scheme the pattern of sounds that repeats at the end of a line or stanza (verse)

rhyming couplets a pattern of rhyme in which lines are written in pairs, and the rhyming pattern is AABBCCDDEE … The pairs of lines rhyme. Shakespeare ends each of his sonnets with a rhyming couplet, but Chaucer wrote thousands of lines of *The Canterbury Tales* in this pattern

rhythm the 'beat' that is created by choice of words, rhyming and number of stressed/unstressed syllables in a line (the meter)

romanticise to make something seem better or more appealing than it really is

scans a poem scans when it follows a regular pattern of stressed and unstressed syllables

scenes *see* **acts**

script the written text of a video, play, film or book

semi-colon (;) links two independent clauses and can be used between sentences that have a common theme to create a pause and emphasis effect, like the effect of a full stop

sentence opener the first word or phrase used in a sentence

setting the place or places in which the events occur

sibilance the repetition of the 's' sound or 'sh' or 'ch' sounds

simile a figure of speech in which two things that are not obviously like each other are compared to make a description more vivid. A simile will often begin with a phrase introduced by 'like' or 'as', e.g. The smoke hung from the chimney like a drooping flag.

slang informal, conversational words or phrases, often peculiar to a particular age group, e.g. It was a *really cool* gig.

sonnet a form of poem that always has 14 lines

stage directions notes to help the actors, often put in brackets or in italics. Actors do not say the stage instructions

standpoint the position from which a writer views and judges things

stanza a verse in a poem which is made up of two or more lines, which often have a common rhyme and pattern

structure the way a text is organised so that it usually has a beginning, middle and end

suffix a letter or group of letters added to the end of a word (or a word stem) in order to form a new word or to alter the grammatical function of the original word

syllable a unit of sound (a beat) that can be a word on its own, e.g. *man*; but can be joined with other units of sound to form words, e.g. *woman*

symbolism using symbols to suggest ideas and qualities

synonym a word that has a similar meaning to another word

theme the content of a text; what a text is about

third-person narration (using 'he', 'she', etc.) the writer shows the thoughts and feelings of several characters

tone what the author feels or wants the reader to feel about something. Tone can be humorous, dark or angry, for example

verb a word that expresses an action or a state of being, e.g. Joe *ate* his dinner. Joe no longer *felt* hungry.

voice an author's unique style of writing; *also* the speaker in a poem (like a narrator in a story)

Acknowledgements

Every effort has been made to trace all copyright holders, but if any have been inadvertently overlooked, the Publishers will be pleased to make the necessary arrangements at the first opportunity.

The publishers would like to thank the following for permission to reproduce copyright material:

Text credits

p.3 'Sparkles from the Wheel' by Walt Whitman. (1900). *Leaves of grass*. D. McKay; **p.7** 'Road to Lacovia' by A.L. Hendriks, © Oxford University Press; **p.9** 'The Road Not Taken' by Robert Frost © Simon & Schuster; **pp.12-13** extract from *The Time Machine* by H.G. Wells, © 1895; **p.15** extract from *In the Company of Cheerful Ladies* by Alexander McCall Smith © Little, Brown Book Group 2004; **p.17** extract from 'The Winter Oak' by Yuri Nagibin, from *Opening Worlds: Short Stories from Different Cultures*,© 2002, Heinemann; **p.19** Pink Lemonade and Cookies' by Kit Kittelstad © 1996-2021 LoveToKnow, Corp.; **pp.28, 30** extracts from *The Diary of a Young Girl* by Anne Frank © 2007. Reproduced by permission of Anne Frank Fonds; **pp.31, 32, 33** extracts from *The Diary of Samuel Pepys*, © Samuel Pepys; **p.84** 'Kyron McMaster wins the British Virgin Islands' first ever medal in perfect tribute to late coach' © The Herald and Weekly Times; **p.85** 'Levern Spencer brings St Lucia its first gold medal at the Commonwealth Games', HTS News 4orce; **pp.87-88** 'Submarine to explore why Antarctic glacier is melting so quickly' by Ian Sample, 28 December, © 2019, Guardian News & Media Limited; **pp.88-89** 'Kids play in Arctic seas as 22°C heatwave grips North Pole at climate change frontline' by Nada Farhoud © MGN Limited; **p.90** extract from *Politics and the English Language* by George Orwell Hardcover Book. United Kingdom: Sahara Publisher Books; **p.92** President John F Kennedy, 1961: speech explaining why the USA would be sending a mission to land on the Moon: https://er.jsc.nasa.gov/seh/ricetalk.htm; First Secretary of State and Secretary of State for Employment and Productivity (Mrs Barbara Castle), during a parliamentary session about a new law to guarantee women and men equal pay, 1970. Contains Parliamentary information licensed under the Open Parliament Licence v3.0. © UK Parliament 2021. Retrieved from http://hansard.millbanksystems.com/people/mrs-barbara-castle; **p.97** *The House in the Mist* by Anna Katharine Green. Bobbs-Merrill Company, 1905; **p.98** Introduction to Bako National Park © MULUNATIONALPARK.COM; What to see at Bako National Park © Sarawak Forestry Corporation; **p.99** Getting there and accommodation © Sarawak Forestry Corporation; **pp.104-105** *Hard Times* by Charles Dickens (1854). Bradbury and Evans; **p.106** 'Where is ...?' by Edith Wharton, from *A Backward Glance* (1934) © 2013 Read Books Ltd.; **p.108** extract from *The Life and Times of the Thunderbolt Kid* by Bill Bryson, ISBN9780385608268, © 2006. Reproduced by permission of The Random House Group Ltd.; **p.110-111** 'Guinness World Records is on a slippery slope' by David Mitchell, July 21, 2019, © Guardian News & Media Limited; **p.115** 'The Snitterjipe' by James Reeves from *Complete Poems For Children*, Faber & Faber © 2014 James Reeves; **p.117** extract from *Alice's Adventures in Wonderland* by Lewis Carroll © 1869 Lee and Shepard; **p.118-119** extract from *The Hobbit* by J.R.R Tolkien © 2012 Houghton Mifflin Harcourt; **p.120** 'The Photo Shoot' by Alison Pitout (Wynberg Girls High School) from *English Alive*, 2010; **p.121** 'Praise Song for My Mother' by Grace Nichols from *The Fat Black Woman's Poems* (Virago, 1984) © Grace Nichols, used by permission of the author; **p.122** 'Mother to Son' by Langston Hughes from *The Collected Works of Langston Hughes* Copyright © 2002 Langston Hughes; **pp.125-126** 'Mending Wall' by Robert Frost © 1969 Henry Holt and Company; **p.129** 'A Blackbird Singing' by R.S. Thomas (1913-2000) © Ronald Stuart Thomas; **p.151** 'Absolution' by Cobus Pienaar, Crawford College Pretoria South Africa © 2012 *English Alive*; **pp.152, 153-154** extracts from pp 22, 24, 25, 26 of *The Return* by Fatima Dike, published by Junkets Publisher; **pp.158-159** extract from The Young Couple' by Ruth Prawer Jhabvala from *A Stronger Climate* © 1968. Reproduced by permission of Maia Publishing Services Ltd.)

Photo credits

p.1 © Kokotewan/stock.adobe.com; **p.2** *l* © christianthiel.net/shutterstock.com, *m* © Belikova Oksana/shutterstock.com, *r* © Jacob Lund/shutterstock.com, *b* © Morphart/stock.adobe.com; **p.3** © The Keasbury-Gordon Photograph Archive/KGPA Ltd/Alamy Stock Photo; **p.4** © 4zevar/stock.adobe.com; **p.7** © Paul Carter Photography/shutterstock.com; **p.14** © Fotokitas/stock.adobe.com; **pp.18–19** © Yanikap/stock.adobe.com; **p.20** © Highwaystarz/stock.adobe.com; **p.21** © flashmovie/stock.adobe.com; **p.23** © Kristina/stock.adobe.com; **p.24** © Ladychelyabinsk/stock.adobe.com; **p.26** *t* © SHOTPRIME STUDIO/stock.adobe.com, *b* © chokniti/stock.adobe.com, *bl* © BullRun/stock.adobe.com, *bm* © Rob Hawkins/Alamy Live News/First Stop Photo/Alamy Stock Photo, *br* © Stephen Lovekin/Shutterstock.com; **p.27** © United Archives GmbH/Alamy Stock Photo; **p.33** © -Misha/stock.adobe.com; **p.34** © Antoine Buchet/Shutterstock.com; **p.35** © Kanpisut/stock.adobe.com; **p.36** © Vectorfusionart/stock.adobe.com; **p.39** © Ruslan Grumble/stock.adobe.com; **p.41** © -Misha/stock.adobe.com; **p.34** © Antoine Buchet/Shutterstock.com; **p.35** © Kanpisut/stock.adobe.com; **p.36** © Vectorfusionart/stock.adobe.com; **p.39** © Ruslan Grumble/stock.adobe.com; **p.41** © vukkostic/stock.adobe.com; **p.42** © matiasdelcarmine/stock.adobe.com. **p.45** © haspil/stock.adobe.com; **p.48** © Astro/stock.adobe.com; **p.50** © AA Film Archive/Alamy Stock Photo; **p.51** © Matiasdelcarmine/stock.adobe.com; **p.54** © David Beauchamp/Shutterstock.com; **p.61** © Scanrail/stock.adobe.com; **p.62** from Parentlineplus, Family Lives www.familylives.org.uk; **p.68** Reproduced by kind permission of Animal Aid; **p.69** *t* © ILYA AKINSHIN/stock.adobe.com; **p.69** *b* © Escapejaja/stock.adobe.com; **p.75** © Monkey Business/stock.adobe.com; **p.84** © Mark Schiefelbein/AP/Shutterstock; **p.85** © Mark Schiefelbein/AP/Shutterstock; **p.79** © Terovesalainen/stock.adobe.com; **p.81** *t* © Watchara tongnoi/stock.adobe.com; **p.81** *b* © I. Pilon/Shutterstock.com; **p.93** © Microgen/stock.adobe.com; **p.99** © Pwollinga/stock.adobe.com; **p.104** [credit to come]; **p.110** © Keith Morris/Alamy Stock Photo; **p.113** © Macrovector/stock.adobe.com; **p.116** ©Library of Congress Prints and Photographs Division [LC-USZ62-70064]; **p.118** © LANDMARK MEDIA/Alamy Stock Photo; **p.120** © Stuart Clarke/Shutterstock.com; **p.122** ©Library of Congress Prints and Photographs Division [LC-USZ62-43605] ; **p.126-7** Way home Studio/stock.adobe.com; **p.129** © Ramn/stock.adobe.com; **p.131** © Archivist/stock.adobe.com; **p.140** *t* © Georgios Kollidas/stock.adobe.com, *b* © Chris Lofty/stock.adobe.com; **p.144** © Caifas/stock.adobe.com; **p.147** © Simone_n/stock.adobe.com; **p.151** © Uremar/stock.adobe.com; **p.152** © Nardus Engelbrecht/Gallo Images/Getty Images; **p.158** © Bernard Gotfryd/Getty Images;

t = top, *b* = bottom, *m* = middle, *l* = left, *r* = right; where there are more than three images together, numbers indicate their position running down the page